In Our Time

Geoffrey Blainey

Published by
Information Australia
A.C.N. 006 042 173
75 Flinders Lane
Melbourne Vic. 3000
Telephone: (03) 9654 2800
Fax: (03) 9650 5261
Internet: www.infoaust.com
Email: mail@infoaust.com

Copyright © 1999

All rights reserved. This publication is copyright and may not be resold or reproduced in any manner (except excerpts thereof for bona fide study purposes in accordance with the Copyright Act) without the prior consent of the Publisher.

Every effort has been made to ensure that this book is free from error or omissions. However, the Publisher, the Authors, the Editor, or their respective employees or agents, shall not accept responsibility for injury, loss or damage occasioned to any person acting or refraining from action as a result of material in this book whether or not such injury, loss or damage is in any way due to any negligent act or omission, breach of duty or default on the part of the Publisher, the Authors, the Editor, or their respective employees or agents.

The National Library of Australia
Cataloguing-in-Publication entry:

Blainey, Geoffrey, 1930-.
  In our time.

ISBN 1 86350 272 6

1. Blainey, Geoffrey, 1930-. 2. Australia - History. 3. Australia - Politics and government - 20th century. 4. Australia - Social conditions - 20th century. 5. Australia - Social life and customs - 20th century. I. Title.

994.04

Page Layout & Design: Ben Graham
Cover Design: Guy Mirabella Design

Printed in Australia by Australian Print Group

Contents

Part 1 – Ranging Over the Past

The Black Armband View of History	3
Have We Lost Our Courage?	15
Will Victoria's History Repeat Itself?	21
The Miracle of the Gallipoli Retreat	27
Billy Hughes and his Momentous Year	31
The Final Months of War	39
1945: The Long Awaited Year	43
Australia and Air Power	55
The Jews Flourished in Australia	63
Did the Forties Mould Australia?	71
Forgetting the Way to Church	81
Does the Future Belong to a Galaxy of Smaller Nations?	85
This Marvellous, Calamitous Century	89
Mr Gibbon's Decline and Fall	93

Part 2 – Partly Personal

The First Christmas I Remember	103
Ballarat	105
Snippet: Who is the Typical Australian?	107
A Few Words at a Funeral	109
Grand Final: the Eagles Win	113
When Football Was Just a Winter Game	117
Ablett	121
Shilling's Worth of Wisdom	125
The Ascent of the Restaurant	129

Part 3 - Themes of the 1990s

Listen to the Footsteps	135
The Gulf War and the Peace Crusade	143
The Plight of the Factory	149
Cyclone Keating	157
Royal Ambitions	161
Aborigines' Losses and Gains	165
Didgeridoo and Kanguru	169
Brain-washing the Children	173
Casino	177
The Violent	181
Australia's Tug O' War: Europe or Asia?	183
What Kind of a Republic?	187
Why the Left Will Rise Again	191

Preface

In 1991 Michael Wilkinson suggested that I bring together under the one cover a collection of some of the articles I had written and speeches made in the previous ten years. Most were about the state of the nation. He then published about sixty of them in a paperback under the title of *Eye on Australia*.

He is it who proposed that I now offer more ready-made ammunition as a gift for my critics. This time he went through maybe 500 articles and speeches and made the selection. It is wider in scope than the previous book and includes articles on burning topics of the day, essays on decades or trends in Australian history, the words I spoke at the funeral of my mother, and one or two snatches of reminiscence. Mr Paul Keating was riding high at the time when I wrote some of the articles. I must say, on reading several of those discussing his government, that some of my views were rather strongly expressed. It is also slightly chastening to see that some events and crises did not turn out as I expected: alas, some did.

Many of the articles were published in the Melbourne *Age*, when I had a Saturday column. Some appeared in the Melbourne *Herald Sun*, the *Bulletin* and *Australian*. Some were written at high speed when an event prompted an editor to ring me up and ask for an article before 4 pm or nightfall. The one on Gary Ablett, the football champion, was written for a pictorial book of which he was the main author. A few were written at the suggestion of Max Suich of the *Independent Monthly* and Bruce Stannard of the *Australian Business Monthly*: sadly both of these monthlies are no more. One essay, on the future of small nations, was written for one of those remarkable conversazioni which Claudio Veliz sponsored at Boston University.

A few of these pieces are far more relevant than when they first appeared. One is the speech – the John Latham memorial lecture – during which I coined the phrase "the black armband view of history". The speech was given in Sydney in the winter of 1993, and at least one daily newspaper published large excerpts from it. The speech aroused interest but, so far as I can remember, no strong criticism or praise. About three years later Mr Howard as prime minister used the phrase in an address at Monash University. Suddenly it took off like a rocket, and became one of the common phrases of public and academic discourse. It is not unfair to say that most public commentators and people of high distinction who attacked the phrase and its meaning had no idea what it signified. Having just read, after six years, my original use of the phrase, I have no reason to alter my views on Australian history nor disown my choice of that phrase. I coined the phrase, incidentally, having at the back of my mind the old custom of Australian Rules football teams to wear a black armband when a club worthy had died.

Occasionally I have corrected some mishap of spelling. In several articles I put back sentences which in their original publication were deleted, presumably through lack of space. Very occasionally I repaired a clumsy sentence. As I often wrote about some of the more gnawing questions of the Nineties, I find that the same point is virtually repeated twice or thrice, though in different words. At the last moment I decided to delete some paragraphs because they spelled out in detail a point or historical analogy already expressed in this book. Of course my conclusions, irrespective of whether or not they now seem sensible, have been left unaltered.

As an author rarely has any say in the headings or titles placed on newspaper articles, I have sometimes given new titles to them. I thank all who commissioned these articles or speeches.

Geoffrey Blainey
August 1999

Part 1
Ranging Over the Past

The Black Armband View of History

What has been good and what has been bad in the history of Australia? I selected this topic because it raises several difficult and dovetailed issues. Moreover, these issues are central in Australian politics and indeed in the nation's own sense of itself and where it is going.

Everyone will draw up a different balance sheet. It will depend partly on the historian's own experience and assumptions and bias. The exact balance sheet depends partly on the year when they happen to draw up the credits and debits, for some years are more buoyant than others. In this short time I will not attempt to draw up a full balance sheet but concentrate on several vital facets of European and also Aboriginal history.

To some extent my generation was reared on the Three Cheers view of history. This patriotic view of our past had a long run. It saw Australian history as largely a success. While the convict era was a source of shame or unease, nearly everything that came after was believed to be pretty good. Now the very opposite is widely preached, especially in the social sciences.

If you first went to school in the 1930s you learned little Australian history but you accepted that the pioneers were at least as worthy as their inheritors. This was the view handed down to the young through school lessons or papers or radio. A nation fighting for its life usually sees that life, present and past, as very much worth defending by persuasion as well as arms. The left wing and the right wing were alike in their congratulations, though they rarely congratulated the same events.

There is a rival view, which I call the Black Armband view of history. In recent years it has assailed the generally optimistic view of Australian history. The black armbands were quietly worn in official circles in 1988, the bicentennial year. Until late in that year Mr Hawke rarely gave a speech that awarded much praise to Australia's history. Even notable Labor leaders from the past - Fisher, Hughes, Scullin, Curtin and Chifley - if listening in their graves in 1988, would have heard virtually no mention of their name and their contributions to the nation they faithfully served. Indeed the Hawke Government excised the earlier official slogan, "The Australian Achievement", replacing it with "Living Together" - a slogan that belongs less to national affairs than to personal affairs. The multicultural folk busily preached their message that until they arrived much of Australian history was a disgrace. The past treatment of Aborigines, of Chinese, of Kanakas, of non-British migrants, of women, the very old, the very young, and the poor was singled out, sometimes legitimately, sometimes not. These condemnations of Australia's past treatment of various categories of people were so sweeping that at times close to eighty per cent of the population was in the "hit list" - a suspiciously high percentage, you must admit, when this was really one of the world's most vigorous democracies.

My friend and undergraduate teacher, Manning Clark, who was almost the official historian in 1988, had done much to spread the gloomy view and also the compassionate view with his powerful prose and his Old Testament phrases. For Manning Clark, Australia was the land where the money-changers had recaptured the temple - a biblical takeover in reverse. Clark spoke of "the sickness of society at large", and the perpetual rule of the tough and the ruthless. Australia, he wrote, is a nation which throughout its history had equated "material achievement with public virtue". These are powerful views, and some evidence can be found to back them, but I do not think, with all respect, that the evidence is strong enough.

Even Australia's material achievements of the past are under the hammer; and some recent books by historians see mainly injustice in the present and poverty and inequality in the past. Why a million people a year were clamouring to enter such an unattractive society, and why so many people had been eager to come across the world in the majority of past decades, was a point not quite explained. Now schoolchildren are often the target for these views. In contrast, the general public for the most part remains proud of the nation's history, or what they know of it - their affection stood out in Sydney on Australia Day, 1988.

To some extent the Black Armband view of history might well represent the swing of the pendulum from a position that had been too favourable, too self-congratulatory, to an opposite extreme that is even more unreal and decidedly jaundiced.

Economic Success or Failure?

Australia - until, say, the last quarter century - was one of the great success stories in the economic history of the world. In the economic realm Australia was more successful 100 years ago than it is today; but it still must be classed as successful. It is in the top 25, using virtually every definition, and by some economic observers it stands in the top 15. Whether such high places will be retained on the world's ladder is difficult to forecast. Australia is likely, on present evidence, to decline further in the next 10 years.

We should measure economic success partly by the steepness of the mountain that had to be climbed. This was a tough country to colonise. I am sure the Aboriginal pioneers found it difficult and in many ways they succeeded. The British also found it difficult. It was far from their homeland. The return voyage was hazardous: the sea route past Cape Horn was the main route from Australia for about 90 years. Australia was probably the finest triumph of long-distance colonisation the world so far had seen.

The newcomers found that the various climates of this continent were strange. The climates remained a riddle. The first settlement at Sydney was made on the basis, understandably, of a blunder about climate. An additional shock was to discover that so much of the continent was arid. This shock was still being felt by explorers in the 1870s. We still do not know what is the typical climate for each Australian region and what is a normal run of seasons.

Australia is the world's largest museum of soil deficiencies. Farming here, compared to North America, was a lottery because the soil, so deficient in phosphate and other minerals, seemed exhausted after only a few crops. Of course the land had natural advantages - sweeping grasslands in which the natural predators were not prolific and a winter climate that did not require the penning of livestock under a roof.

All in all, it was a great achievement to turn Australia into one of the world's great producers of foods and fibres. The natural fibres are costlier and less in favour in this era of synthetic fibres but in the cold winters of the Northern Hemisphere, how many hundreds of millions of lives were made more livable or even prolonged by Australian wool? Likewise Australian-grown food is not so urgently needed at present but its era will probably come again. Meanwhile, in a reasonably favourable year of the last decade Australia was probably producing enough food to sustain - on a modest intake of calories - close to 100 million people here and overseas. That is a remarkable achievement in a continent where probably fewer than one million people could feed themselves in Aboriginal times.

The story of mineral production in Australia needs no comment, except to say that it depends more on effort, imagination and efficiency than on luck. If luck really is all-important, why did the Aborigines have so little luck as miners? The phrase "lucky country" is plainly misleading when applied unthinkingly to any primary industry, let alone to the whole economy.

When you place the obstacles on one side and the economic achievements on the other, you have to give three cheers - or if you are mean, two and a half. It is true, as many critics point out, that the wealth produced has not been evenly spread. At the same time those regimes which, like the Soviet Union, claim to have been successful in spreading wealth have failed dismally to produce enough wealth to spread. For most of the last 100 years it was better to be a poor Australian than a middle-income member of most other nations.

The heyday of Australia's economic success was in the period from the end of the first gold boom to about the eve of the First World War. The late Professor N.G. Butlin of the Australian National University placed Australia's living standards at the top of the world at about the start of this century, and this verdict is passing proudly into Australian folklore. It is difficult to know whether this verdict is valid: international comparisons are so hazardous. I myself would call it a powerfully argued guess. Moreover, his calculations excluded the Aborigines. At the same time, Australians almost certainly stood on one of the top four rungs of the world's ladder of prosperity in most years from 1870 to 1914.

Why has Australia, while still standing high on the world's economic ladder, been forced to step down many rungs? A significant part of the descent took place in the last decade, and can be explained by poor economic management, more in Canberra but also in the tall glasshouses of Melbourne, Sydney, Adelaide, Perth and Brisbane. But the major descent from the top rungs of the ladder began even earlier. Two reasons for the relative decline between 1914 and 1950 were geographical. In a period when the world moved steadily from firewood and coal towards oil, we lacked our own supply of oil: so an energy-rich country lost its advantage. Moreover, the climate in south-eastern Australia, so important to the rural economy, was relatively dry.

Over a longer period, our economic decline owes much to cultural factors reinforced by political decisions: a reluctance to save money, partly because of the increase in social security; a high preference for leisure; and a work culture which is more laid-back than our powerful and vigorous sports culture. The difference between our Friday and our Saturday values is almost a cultural iron curtain.

A Scoreboard of Ecology

Beyond dispute, the colonising of Australia since 1788 has done great damage to the environment, mostly in the areas of urban and agricultural settlement. What we call economic progress took place with such speed and with such scant knowledge of the environment. There was a heavy toll, including the destruction of rare species of plants and animals, the increasing salinity of irrigated lands, the clearing of forests, and the deliberate introduction of new animals - rabbit, cat, fox and many others - that displaced or preyed on native species. On the basis of damage for each 100 square kilometres, we cannot feel sure whether greater alteration was made to Australia than to Europe in the last 200 years, though in the last 2000 years Europe has probably been altered the more, simply because of the sheer density of its human settlement.

There are various ways of measuring comparative ecological damage just as there are of defining democracy. Do you apportion the blame for ecological damage partly by counting the damage done in relation to the number of lives lived in the region, or the damage done for each 1000 square kilometres of a nation's territory, or the relative vulnerability of the environment to damage of certain kinds? For example, a small population occupying a large area that is not very vulnerable does not necessarily deserve high marks for inflicting less harm on the species and landscape. No doubt the settled regions of south-eastern Australia are one of the world's areas damaged the most in a short space of time. Admittedly, it was one of the more vulnerable areas, even before the First Fleet arrived. The Aboriginal record of damage was also high, when one considers their simple technology and the fact that so few new species were introduced in addition to human beings and dingoes.

Democracy

I count democracy as one of the major credits on the national balance sheet. Australia was an early convert. By 1860, the overwhelming majority of Australia's population lived in democratic territory - Western Australia and most of the Aboriginal people were the exception. I guess I'm the originator of the statement, now creeping into wider usage, that Australia is one of the five or six oldest continuous democracies in the world, but I am only too aware that it is one of those statements that passes muster so long as it is not inspected too closely. After all, what is a democracy? What was called a democracy in the time of Disraeli or Bismarck might not be called one today. What proportion of adults must possess the right to vote if their land is to be called a democracy? If 50 per cent is required, then there was no democracy in the history of the world even as late as 1890.

Even when nearly all the adult men had the right to vote in the election of representatives to a lower house - and Australia had reached that stage by the 1860s - their ultimate power, and their legitimate title to the word democracy, was in effect limited by a variety of countervailing powers. The checks and limits included the monarchy and its colonial representative who was the governor. They included the power to conduct foreign policy (a power largely residing in Westminster), the courts, a restrictive upper house and uneven electorates. Even allowing for the variety of such checks which operated in virtually all European or colonial democracies as late as 1890, and even allowing for the different checks operating in the republic of the United States (including the fact of slavery), Australia is by any reasonable definition one of the oldest continuous democracies in the world. The word *continuous* is important because many European democracies were crushed by Hitler.

There is a valid case for arguing that Australia is the oldest continuous democracy in the world, for in 1903 it became the first national Parliament to permit women both to vote and to stand for election. I did not hear in the bicentennial year of 1988 our national leaders refer even once to this long and remarkable democratic achievement of the country they were allegedly celebrating.

In Australia democracy is less in favour in intellectual circles today than 30 years ago. The more emphasis that is placed on the rights of minorities, and the need for affirmative action to enhance those rights, the more is the concept of democracy - and the rights of the majority – in danger of being weakened. Likewise, the High Court in recent years might be seen as a quiet challenger to democracy. At times it is beginning to see itself as a third and very powerful house in the Federal system of government. The 1988 referendum, fortunately rejected, was a subtle attempt by the Federal Government to increase those powers.

Australia won democracy with relative ease in a series of bloodless steps. We tend to take it for granted and to think that it is an easy system to operate. It is not, however, so easily operated. In fact it depends partly on a society which emphasises individual responsibility as much as individual rights. We became a rights-mad society in the 1970s and 1980s, forgetting that there will never be enough rights to go around. A firm right granted to one person or group is often a loss of a right to another person or group. The Bill of Rights that nearly passed through the Federal Parliament in

1986 was a traffic jam of competing rights. It would be unwise, indeed complacent, to see democracy as a permanent victory for Australia.

The Aborigines

Many Australians see the treatment of Aborigines, since 1788, as the blot on Australian history. Fifty years ago, fewer than 50,000 Australians probably saw this as the blot. Now maybe several million are convinced that it is the main blot and maybe half of the population, or even more, would see it as highly regrettable. Irrespective of whether deep shame or wide regret is the more appropriate response, this question will be here to vex or torment the nation for a long time to come.

My own view on this question is much influenced by my own particular interpretation of Australian history. My starting point you might disagree with, but I have held it for some 20 years, have often reconsidered it, and will hold on to it until contrary evidence arrives.

The meeting of the incoming British with the Aborigines, at a thousand different parts of Australia spread over more than a century, was possibly a unique confrontation in recorded history. No doubt a version of the episode happened somewhere else, hundreds of years earlier, on a smaller scale. But there is probably no other historical parallel of a confrontation so strange, so puzzling to both sides, and embracing such a huge area of the world's surface. If we accept this fact we begin to understand the magnitude of the problem that appeared in 1788, puzzled Governor Arthur Phillip, a man of goodwill, and is still with us. It will probably remain with us for the foreseeable future, defying the variety of quick-fix formulas that sometimes attract the Federal Government, tempt the High Court, and tantalise thoughtful Aboriginal leaders.

In 1788, the world was becoming one world. Europe's sailing ships had entered nearly every navigable sea and strait on the globe, and the ships' crews were alert for anything that was trade-able, and so they were sure to return to any place of promise. In 1788, the industrial revolution was also beginning. Here landed representatives of the nation which had just developed the steam engine, the most powerful machine the world had known, and also the semi-mechanised cotton mill. On the other hand Australia represented the way of life that almost certainly prevailed over the whole habitable globe some 10,000 years earlier. The Aborigines had no domesticated plants and animals and therefore a very different attitude to the land - this is part of the long painful background to the Mabo Case. They had no pottery, they had implements of wood and bone and stone but none of metals, they had no paper and no writing, though they were skilled at a variety of other signs. They had no organisation embracing more than say 3,000 people and probably no organisation capable of putting more than 200 people into a battlefield at the one time. They had few, if any, permanent villages, and only a token ability to hoard food. They believed in a living, intervening god - here was a close resemblance - but not the God seen as the correct one. It was a society with many distinctive merits, often overlooked, but it was startlingly different to the one that supplanted it.

In 1788, Aboriginal Australia was a world almost as remote, as different as outer space. We now think of Aboriginal Australia as having a unity, but it had even less unity than Europe possesses today. There were countless economic and social differences, and an amazing variety of languages. Accordingly the idea, widely voiced now, that the incoming British could have - and should have - signed a treaty with *the* Aborigines, and so worked out rights and compensations, rests on a faith in the impossible. Any treaty would have been one-sided, with the Aborigines as losers.

Even if the First Fleet had brought out not the dross but the wisest and most humane women and men in England, and even if the Aborigines whom they met at Sydney Harbour were the wisest of all their people, how conceivably could a treaty have been signed - given the differences in language and understanding? And if a treaty were signed, how far inland and along the coast would it have extended? The north and south sides of Sydney Harbour, then as now, had different languages and tribal arrangements. (I do not use this argument, incidentally, to comment on the question of whether there should or should not be a treaty today.) There was a huge contrast between the two cultures, the incoming and the resident. Every Australian still inherits the difficult consequence of that contrast.

How can we fairly summarise this complex and delicate question: was the treatment of Aborigines an ineradicable stain on Australian history? There are many answers, each of them a part answer.

The Aborigines probably enjoyed a very high standard of living, so long as their population remained low. My belief - I have set it out elsewhere - is that they were a highly successful society in the economic sphere, and that the typical Aborigines in 1788 had a more varied and more secure diet than the typical Europeans. This kind of semi-nomadic society once existed everywhere in the inhabitable world, but in the years of the neolithic revolution it had vanished from every large land mass except Australia. A highly skilled system, it was extravagant - and we are too - in the use of space and land and resources. A huge area was needed to support few people. Such were the land needs that the whole globe in the time of the hunters and gatherers perhaps supported only one per cent of its present population.

Such a form of land use was bound to be overthrown or undermined. The world's history has depended heavily on the eclipse of this old and wasteful economic way of life - wasteful in terms of human potential though not wasteful in terms, modern terms, of the whole range of living things. There is no way it could be preserved. The miracle is that it survived until 1788 and later. It was tragic for the generation that had to lose it. Any idea that the Aboriginal way of life of 1788 could have been retained for centuries more is a daydream. It is strange that the Australian version of land rights almost tries to restore this archaic and untenable way of life.

After the British arrived, the treatment of Aborigines was often lamentable: the frequent contempt for their culture, sometimes the contempt for the colour of their skin, the removal of their freedoms and usually the breaking of their precious link with their tribal homelands. And also the killing of them, in ones and tens and even occasionally in the hundred. In 150 years it may be that as many as 20,000 Aborigines were killed, predominantly by Europeans but sometimes by Aborigines enrolled as troopers.

After many attempts to help Aborigines, it came to be widely believed by about 1850 that nothing effective could be done to preserve or rescue them. So dramatically were their numbers declining that they were expected by learned opinion in Europe and the Americas to die out. Learned opinion was mistaken. Interestingly, this mistaken view was in part self-serving but it was the considered view of science at a time when science was being enthroned as king. Charles Darwin, the greatest biological scientist of his day, believed that the Aborigines were doomed. It is ironical that science, which transformed Australia and made it so productive, was so astray on a matter so vital to the Aborigines.

Oddly, the vilification of Aborigines by Europeans who lived in the 19th century is now almost matched by the vilification of those same Europeans at the hands of presentday moralists, scholars, journalists and film-makers. Again and again we see and hear the mischievous statements that the Aborigines' numbers were drastically reduced primarily by slaughter. In fact, diseases were the great killer by a very large margin.

It is also timely to recall that the loss of life in traditional Aboriginal society - whether through infanticide or through warfare and other kinds of violence - was probably on a large scale. There is a tendency today to treat traditional Aboriginal society as especially peace-loving, a view to which I do not at present subscribe, though the evidence is sparse. The Aborigines were and are human beings with the same capacity as Europeans to live in peace or to make war. At present there is a tendency, maybe a welcome tendency, not to look too closely at traditional Aboriginal society. Certainly it was grossly over-criticised in the past. At the same time, it is unwise and unfair if the temporary drawing of the blinds over that society is accompanied by crude propaganda directed at the equally vulnerable European society which pushed aside the Aborigines.

Even on recent issues the accounts of the treatment of Aborigines have little relation to fact. How often, for example, do we now hear it said that the Aborigines had no vote until 1967? Credit should be given for attempts to redress past wrongs.

It is not easy to draw rules for the handling of such explosive questions. We have to try, however, to be fair to both sides - the early Australians and the Europeans who arrived later. Understanding is needed on all sides, and neither I, nor anybody else, can claim an adequate understanding of such a complicated and unusual question. Nothing does less to promote discussion than the constant use of the word racist. It is often a correct word but it is also becoming the favourite word of the prejudiced, the ignorant, and often the intellectually unscrupulous.

Anyone who tries to range over the last 200 years of Australia's history, surveying the successes and failures, and trying to understand the obstacles that stood in the way, cannot easily accept the gloomier summaries of that history. Some episodes in the past were regrettable, there were many flaws and failures, and yet on the whole it stands out as one the world's success stories. It is ironical that many of the political and intellectual leaders of the last decade, one of the most complacent and disappointing decades in our history, are so eager to denounce earlier generations and discount their hard-won successes.

Most young Australians, irrespective of their background, are quietly proud to be Australian. We deprive them of their inheritance if we claim that they have inherited little to be proud of.

Quadrant, July - August, 1993

Have We Lost Our Courage?

Bravery is probably one of the minor casualties of modern Australia. It is still here in impressive quantities - it was present in a quiet way amongst some victims and rescuers at Port Arthur - but it is not valued quite as highly as it was.

In pioneering Australia, most people ranked bravery as the highest of the virtues. Schoolbooks sang the praises of the brave and the public donated their shillings to set up monuments.

In what was once Australia's best-known verse, Adam Lindsay Gordon insisted that two things stood like stone - "kindness in another's trouble, courage in your own". A fine steeplechase rider, he was full of courage when he rode on Victorian racecourses - until his own fears and miseries made him commit suicide by a beach near Melbourne in 1870. One reason for his fame was that he said what a pioneering country liked to hear.

Disasters in Australia's early days took away lives, in proportion to the population, on a massive scale. Australia's worst civilian disaster took place in winter 1845 when a sailing ship, nearing the end of her voyage from Liverpool to Melbourne, was wrecked on King Island near the entrance to Bass Strait. A total of 399 were drowned. Australia today would have to suffer an earthquake or a tropical cyclone killing say 24,000 people in order to lose, with one blow, a comparable percentage of the nation's present population.

It might not always have been a land fit for heroes but it provided them with plenty of opportunity. The floods were devastating in the era when bridges were few, when rivers rose suddenly without a warning sent from people upstream, and when few of the inland settlers could swim. A flood at Gundagai in 1852 cost the lives of 89.

The acts of bravery, often unrecorded, when ships were wrecked or floods or bushfires came through, must have run into thousands even before 1850.

The Murrumbidgee and Murray were scenes of acts of bravery, decade after decade. One of the remarkable rescuers was William Moon of Gundagai. About three decades after the big flood he rescued a boy from drowning and then eight months later he rescued another. He was aged seven at the time of his first exploit in 1887. In river tragedies many heroic rescuers were dragged under by the person about to be saved.

For the first time it is possible to see a wide range of these brave acts because Colin Bannister this week has published his history of the Royal Humane Society of Australasia, which he calls *7000 Brave Australians*. A fascinating catalogue of courage, it also reveals how the forms of bravery have changed since the origins of the society in 1874

Drownings have inspired the biggest number of rewarded acts of courage in Australia, with the surf and the ocean replacing inland water as the main settings for those episodes.

A century ago, runaway horses and goring bulls called for deeds of bravery. Catching frightened horses was a frequent necessity in the streets of horse-drawn cities, and in Melbourne the corner at Flinders Street railway station witnessed many acts of bravery. The early era of the motor car, curiously, multiplied these deeds, the noisy car possibly frightening the horses.

The long-standing Australian award for civilian bravery is the Clarke Medal, and it was first awarded to a 22-year-old Tasmanian yachtsman, Henry Hall, for a brave rescue in Bass Strait in the winter of 1882. Its forerunner, simply called the Gold Medal, was first awarded to Tom Pearce who was the hero in the wreck of the *Loch Ard* near the cliffs of Port Campbell (Vic.) in June 1878.

At one time sinkers of wells and miners working underground were persistent winners of the Clarke. Between 1892 and 1902, the medal was awarded just seven times, and at least four of the recipients were gold miners, including William Rogers and James Tonkin of Eaglehawk (Vic.) who were heroes in separate mining mishaps, and Maurice Doody and Charles Hicks from the Kalgoorlie district.

The first woman to gain the medal was Lavinia Kennedy, aged 40, the wife of a railway worker in upcountry Victoria. In December 1908 she ran to snatch a child from the path of an approaching train. She succeeded, but she was close to death when the wheels of the train swished over her hair, her head being only nine inches away from the rail.

The largest number of medals and commendations to be awarded by the Royal Humane Society of Australasia for the one disaster sprang from the fire in the North Mount Lyell copper mine in western Tasmania in October 1912. A host of miners were trapped underground by smoke and fumes, and 42 men lost their lives. Awards went to 34 men who made or attempted rescues.

Some hazards remain, occasioning bravery decade after decade. Rescues of victims of sharks and crocodiles are prominent in the records, and indeed in two successive years in the 1950s the Clarke Medal was awarded to the heroes of shark attacks, Omi-Tavua on Bougainville Island and Allan Bradford of Surfers Paradise.

It should be said that national records of bravery suffer a little because of the split between the national society based in Victoria and the NSW society which went its own way in 1909 and cultivated its own territory.

There have always been mad bullies holding guns at victim's heads but only in the last decade have their guns been so devastating. In the period from 1901 to 1920 the Royal Humane Society recognised bravery in only one incident that involved weapons, but in the 13 years between 1981 and 1994 there were 33 such incidents.

One of the highest awards ever given to an Australian was the Stanhope Medal which is awarded once a year for the finest act of bravery in the British Commonwealth. It was awarded, along with the Clarke Medal, to Betty Ellen Smith who deliberately confronted a beserk gunman who entered the Mercy Hospital in East Melbourne in November 1992.

My reading of history is that bravery is less valued by Australians today than in 1900, and that there must be side effects from this slow swing in values. Maybe in each month a few rescues, which otherwise might be made, are not even attempted because the courage to act quickly is absent or dimmed.

Of course there is still abundant bravery, just waiting for something to happen, inside hundreds of thousands of Australians; but those who act are not adequately recognised or rewarded. There is now an Australian hall of fame for almost everything except civilian bravery and sheer self-sacrifice, and yet this was perhaps the greatest of the traditional virtues and was displayed mostly by ordinary Australians coming from every walk of life. The Clarke Medal, sadly, has no magic compared to the Brownlow or an Olympic gold medal, but some say that it should stand almost alongside the Victoria Cross.

There must be reasons for our tendency now to take bravery more for granted. In contrast, a pioneering society placed an exceptional value on bravery. Its people faced floods and shipwrecks and other hazards of nature, whereas most of us are not pioneers. Likewise, self-help was seen as a special virtue in those days, but today we often expect the government to rescue us. It would be interesting to know whether the police are now expected to carry out more rescues than in the past. They certainly now appear again and again in the list of the brave.

It could be that a rural society rather than a big city was more likely to praise bravery. A big city can be impersonal and its people possibly feel less of an obligation towards others. If this is true, then the relative decline of rural life will have effects on the frequency of acts of bravery across the nation.

It is true that the two world wars instilled a respect for bravery amongst Australians, and we have not been in a major war for half a century. I doubt, however, whether the long absence of a major war has helped bravery to be less admired. Bravery was seen as a virtue long before Gallipoli and the Battle of the Somme. It struck me recently that one reason why Gallipoli so caught the imagination of Australians was that bravery had for so long stood high on the list of their virtues.

Some would say that the oldtime emphasis on bravery was a sign that Australia used to be unduly masculine in its attitudes but I am not sure whether this argument is relevant. Bravery and self-sacrifice probably were prized equally by women. Much of the quiet bravery in Australia was that of women. And if a nation comes to devalue bravery even a little, then women and children will often be the losers.

Weekend Australian, 25-26 May, 1996

IN OUR TIME

Will Victoria's History Repeat Itself?

The boom in Victoria in the "marvellous" 1880s and the Melbourne boom a century later have a lot in common. But if a warning lesson is still to be learnt, it must come from the devastating slump of the 1890s.

Melbourne's worst year was 1893. Distress was so widespread that scores of churches set aside Wednesday, 17 May as a "day of humiliation and prayer". The Anglican Archbishop called on his flock to attend church on that week day and take part in the service normally used on Ash Wednesday. For most people of that era, a day of prayer was the equivalent of a one-day strike.

The city was partly paying the price for the cocktail of excitement and error it had drunk in the 1880s, when its population grew from less than 300,000 to nearly 500,000 — the equivalent of our Melbourne growing in the next 10 years from three million to five million. So many blocks of land had been sold during boom years that some subdivisions as far away as Laverton were not built on for another 60 years. So many houses were built that some suburbs had street after street of new houses, nearly all of which remained empty for many years.

In 1893, the glut of city offices was also acute. Melbourne owned a cluster of new baby skyscrapers, especially on the lower slopes of Queen Street, which were taller than any office buildings in Europe. The pride of Victoria, the Australian Building, standing in gaunt brick on the north-west corner of Flinders Lane and Elizabeth Street, was too large for the dwindling market for office space. Eight years after its grand opening it was still trying to find tenants for two-thirds of its rooms. Today the city has a similar glut of offices, though no glut of suburban houses.

For Victorians, 1893 was long remembered because most of the banks had to close their doors for many weeks. After they reopened, they virtually had to freeze part of the public's deposits for months or even years. A central bank, had it existed, could have prevented most of those banks from closing because they were probably more solvent than the State Bank of Victoria in its last gasp in 1992. The idea of a central bank had been shunned in the boom years of the 1880s because no financial crisis was predicted. "It can't happen here" was the frequent saying in business circles and in Parliament House. The saying was again common a few years ago.

Victoria was in more misery than it is today. There was no dole and no old-age pension. Social security did not extend far beyond the smell of the soup kitchen in public halls and city lanes. There were no official unemployment figures, but in Melbourne the percentage may have exceeded 20 per cent.

Northcote, then a new suburb, was a casualty of 1893. It depended on the claypits and kilns that had made bricks for booming Melbourne. With few new orders, they now employed 100 men, instead of 500. Almost one in four shops in Northcote fell vacant. In some of its outlying areas, a quarter of the houses were empty. The brass band was dissolved, the bandsmen had gone elsewhere to look for work.

After a clergyman had talked about Northcote's poverty while visiting the country, the town of Casterton railed boxes of bread and meat as a gift to Northcote. At least one old man died of starvation, too proud to ask for charity. Even charity was tightly rationed and at least nine months before the depth of the depression the local Benevolent Society had to stop giving help to families of the unemployed because it was swamped by demands from the sick and the old.

Overall, country towns were hit less than Melbourne — the opposite is probably true today. In winter a rural resident could at least chop firewood or catch rabbits. In many districts they could look for gold, the output of which rose quickly. The Bendigo mines enjoyed a mild boom in the depression of the 1890s.

Will Victoria's History Repeat Itself?

The Victorian Government pruned everything that could be snipped. It closed the lavish new teachers' college at the top end of Swanston Street. It cut all salaries. It made wealthier Victorians pay their first income tax.

It would be rash to make too many contrasts between their depression and ours, but one likeness does exist. In 1893, as now, Victoria was initially hit harder than the rest of Australia. Moreover, we run the risk of repeating their long-term outflow of population, and that's a dangerous economic trend.

People poured out of Melbourne in the 1890s. Melbourne soon lost to Sydney the title of Australia's largest city. Such was the outflow, mainly by ship, that in the 15 years after 1891, Victoria lost through migration more people than it had gained by migration in the previous 30 years. That must be one of the most sobering statistics in Victorian history.

Western Australian goldfields were a haven for Victorians who had no jobs and little money. In certain weeks, as many as four crowded passenger ships left the wharves along the Yarra River for the WA ports. At the large new Coolgardie state school, nearly all the children were Victorians. The main source of income in some Victorian townships was money orders arriving from Kalgoorlie and other gold towns.

Remittances by the hundreds came from Johannesburg, where enough Victorians settled to set up a small league of Australian Rules football. Every South African city had its colony of Victorians, and the best reading rooms in Transvaal and Natal libraries tended to subscribe to the Melbourne weeklies. In 1970 in Durban I met by chance an old man who had emigrated from Gippsland as a boy and had never revisited. He was curious to know whether Essendon was winning the football — he imagined they still played on the vanished East Melbourne ground — and was surprised to learn that the Outer Circle Railway had ceased to run and that the cable trams had gone from Bourke Street.

Much talent left Victoria in search of opportunity during the 20 years after the bank crashes. A few people in Benalla must have wondered whatever happened to that young Michael Savage, who used to work as a lad in a local wine and spirits store and run with the hoses for the local fire brigade. In 1935 the name of Savage reached the headlines, as the first Labor Prime Minister of New Zealand.

So many primary schools were closed that teachers in their hundreds were redundant. J. T. Ryan, son of a Port Fairy farmer, left the state to teach Latin in Launceston and later in Queensland. People who hadn't heard of him for years wondered in 1915 whether he was the Ryan — daily papers printed no photographs then — who had just become Premier of Queensland; he certainly was. Likewise, Philip Collier, son of a farmer just north of Melbourne, went west to Boulder City in 1904 to work in the Perseverance mine, and just 20 years later he began his long period as premier of Western Australia, sitting in a House sprinkled with members who had learned to read in Victorian school rooms.

A few Victorians had returned from exile to win office in their home state. In every year from the onset of the world depression to the end of the Second World War, the Premier of Victoria was a homecomer: E. J. Hogan, who earned enough as a union man in the woodcutters' camps near Kalgoorlie to buy a farm back in his native Ballarat district; Sir Stanley Argyle who studied medicine in London but came home after the bank crashes cut off his funds; and Albert Dunstan, who took up farming on the Darling Downs before returning to Victoria.

So many young men left Victoria that the statistician recorded a fact that astonished people. In a land where the males always outnumbered the females (even in 1830 the ratio was 3-to-1 in favor of the males), Victoria became the first state, and for years the only state, where the females were more numerous. Victoria now had an old population by Australian standards. For decades Victoria was to have the lowest birth rate.

Every skilled trade, every profession from the law to the church, and every branch of sport displayed the same exodus from once-proud Victoria. In billiards saloons — Victoria had hundreds — the income fell and many keepers moved away. So the future genius of the game, Walter A. Lindrum, the son of a billiards-saloon keeper, was born not in Port Melbourne but in Kalgoorlie, as his initials "W. A." proclaimed.

Victoria recovered, with a mixture of firm steps and stumbles, from its depression of the 1890s. After being tripped by a fierce drought, it was definitely prosperous by about 1906. It had helped to restore its own prosperity by leading the campaign to form the Commonwealth of Australia, and as a reward it was the site of the temporary Federal capital from 1901 and its factories were the chief recipient of the protective tariff imposed by the new Federal Parliament.

To Victorian patriots, however, it was only a half recovery. The population of other states continued to grow at a faster percentage. In every five-year period from 1891 to 1921, Victoria was a laggard, and thrice it sat at the bottom of the interstate table and twice it was second last, having lost too many of its sons and daughters to other states.

Today, Victoria is seeing another, quieter exodus, especially of retirees heading for the Queensland coast. In the short term, the outflow is accelerated by Victorians retrenched from railways, schools and other offices in the public sector, and so some critics insist that retrenchments should cease. The answer is that in the Cain years, the public sector grew more rapidly than the state could afford. Therefore the Victorian Government has little alternative but to reduce, at the worst possible time, what should have been tackled a few years ago when times were easier and the fallout from job losses would have been lighter.

One cause for concern is that even before Victoria ran into debt in the 1980s, it was losing economic momentum. From the end of the Second World War until, say, the late 1960s — the heyday of the Australian factory — Victoria's population had grown at a faster rate than that of its main rival, New South Wales. In the past 20 years, however, Victoria has not kept pace with NSW, and the present financial crisis will further shackle Victoria. Even worse is the comparison with Perth and Brisbane, which have been growing in many years at nearly three times the pace of Melbourne.

As Victoria, in its rate of growth, wasn't doing very well in the years when all Australia was prosperous, it can least of all expect to compete with other states in the leaner times. Its strongest hope is in tourism but its record here has been lacklustre. The evidence is strong that in Australia in the next 20 years, tourism will create far more jobs than even manufacturing created in the era of Curtin, Chifley and Menzies. Victoria has to snatch its full share of those tourist jobs, or it could flounder.

Combining with other states, it also should use political strength to withdraw a proportion of Federal public-sector jobs from that over-powerful city, Canberra. It needs to produce the cheapest possible electricity, it has to make Tullamarine compete more with Mascot, it has to provide smoother industrial relations, it somehow has to make its streets and houses less vulnerable to violence and robbery. The list is long but not impossible.

Victoria is again at a crossroads. If it turns in the wrong direction — or does not turn at all — it is in danger of repeating the damaging exodus of the 1890s depression. Admittedly, many people will point out that Victoria's roads will be less congested, and the city smog and bay pollution will be lower, and the Dandenongs might remain intact if population grows slowly. And they are probably right.

But if Victoria grows too slowly they will also find that their own chances of a job or the kind of job they prefer are smaller, that friends and family are more likely to move interstate, and that Victorian cultural and sporting life loses some of its vitality. Even football fans will find that in a stagnant or slow-growing Victoria, a few of the old teams quietly die, to be replaced by clones from the new-money states.

The Age, 13 February, 1993

The Miracle of the Gallipoli Retreat

The landing at Gallipoli is still celebrated but the abandoning of Gallipoli has passed from memory. In some ways the retreat from Gallipoli was the more remarkable event, and but for its miraculous outcome I doubt whether Australians would ever have resolved to celebrate Anzac Day as a national holiday.

The decision to abandon Gallipoli was on the cards not long after the first landing had failed to achieve the quick victory anticipated. Six months after landing, some 140,000 British, French, Australian and New Zealand troops were barely clinging to the tiny zones they had won along the Turkish coast. Both sides had dug in. The fighting was utterly deadlocked.

Neither the Turks nor the Allies had much chance of breaking through the opponents' trenches and fortifications, even at the cost of tens of thousands of additional lives. So in October 1915, the Allies began to think seriously of abandoning the beaches, hills and gullies. It was clear that all these troops could be used effectively in France or another fighting front. Furthermore, outside the ranks of the Australian and New Zealand Army Corps, morale and fighting fitness were patchy.

In order to maintain the armed forces on Gallipoli in the coming winter, an enormous quantity of goods would have to be shipped from Britain to the Mediterranean and landed on the exposed beaches — 10,000 oil stoves to warm the troops at night, a mountain of winter clothing and gum boots, 5000 tons of corrugated iron for the building of winter shelters, hundreds of pumps so that rainwater could be pumped from deep trenches where the soldiers sheltered, and loads of road metal so that, when rain fell, the muddy tracks and roads to the frontlines could be made firmer.

As the proposal to abandon Gallipoli was being debated secretly by the war cabinet in London, the weather on the battle front became all-important. On days of strong south-westerlies, no supplies could be safely landed at the makeshift ports on Gallipoli. Towards the end of November the weather briefly became cold and stormy. In the Suvla zone more than 200 soldiers were either frozen to death or were drowned when the trenches became flooded. In three days there were 5000 cases of frostbite, even before winter had begun.

If the armies were to be evacuated, they would have to embark secretly at night, without giving as much as a hint of warning to the nearby Turks. The Allied soldiers could leave in the small boats only in fine weather. And what would happen if much of the army was successfully evacuated but then the wind rose, thus closing the harbors and leaving a remaining force of say 25,000 Australian, British, New Zealand, Senegal and other soldiers at the mercy of a Turkish army five times as numerous?

General Sir Ian Hamilton, in charge of Gallipoli, was asked to report on the dangers of an evacuation. He privately predicted that maybe 70,000 troops could be lost if the weather changed or the plan misfired. He saw a risk of the greatest military catastrophe in Britain's long history. Others shared his fears. Early in December, however, the risky decision was taken. From Anzac Cove and Suvla Bay, the first soldiers, horses and mules were quietly evacuated during the long nights, while a massive embarkation was secretly planned for 18 and 19 December.

As if by a miracle, the icy storms of late November were followed by weeks of continuously calm and sunny weather — almost like the Easter that has just passed. On the two crucial nights, the sea was almost like a mirror. At daybreak on 20 December, 1915, a morning of thick mist, all that remained near Anzac Cove were 70 abandoned mules and donkeys. That evening the weather broke.

On Gallipoli, 7,600 Australians lost their life. If the Turks had got wind of the secret evacuation and planned accordingly, or if the sea had become rough at the wrong time, or if the retreat had not been planned with skill and subterfuge by General Brudenell White at Anzac Cove, and by other naval and military officers, then the total Australian deaths on Gallipoli could have been doubled. Such a disaster might well have wiped away the pride and sense of purpose aroused by the successful landing on 25 April, thus forcing the nation to select a very different day of remembrance.

The Age, 24 April, 1993

IN OUR TIME

Billy Hughes and his Momentous Year

The cable announcing the end of the First World War reached Melbourne, the Federal capital, at 7. 20 pm on Monday, 11 November, 1918. The news was posted on noticeboards outside the newspaper offices, and it was swiftly spread by word of mouth. Relief and excitement, often tinged with grief, took over every capital city: the bush was yet to hear the news.

It seemed that Australia could retreat from the entanglements of the world, once it brought home all the soldiers and sailors, nurses, stretcher-bearers, aviators, doctors, prisoners of war and others who were in Europe and at sea. And yet in the following months, Australia jumped, as never before, onto the world stage.

William Morris Hughes was the Prime Minister on the day the war ended. Called "The Little Digger" by those who admired him, he received other names from those who mistrusted him. But nobody could deny his talent and sheer determination. He had risen from nothing.

Born in the inner London suburb of Pimlico, the only child of Welsh parents of no wealth, he was moved to a small Welsh farm after his mother died. Later teaching school in London, he saw no future, and sailed at the age of 22 to Brisbane as an assisted migrant. He worked in the outback and cooked in a coastal ship before moving to Sydney where he became a jack-of-all-trades.

He could mend an umbrella, serve in his new wife's tiny shop, carry a soapbox to a street corner in Balmain, or organise a waterfront dispute. When in 1894 he won a Sydney seat on behalf of the infant Labor Party, his supporters bought him a new suit so that he could appear neat.

A neat appearance he hardly needed. He had wit and a flair for words, though his voice did acquire that harshness common amongst those who addressed rowdy crowds in the open air. He spoke fluently and urgently on defence and nearly every other topic, adding a sense of timing as he gained experience. In his heyday he was to be the most electrifying of speech-makers, being called "a rare spellbinder" by Dr Earle Page of the new Country Party, who was not exactly his unbounded admirer.

"Billy" Hughes sat in the first Federal Parliament in Melbourne, becoming Minister for External Affairs in that first brief Labor ministry of 1904, and winning enemies with his biting personal attacks and friends with his humour. Photographs of him show a small figure - probably less than five feet six in height - with big ears, a clipped moustache, and a thin elfin face that was ever so eager. Cartoons depicted him as a gnome or mouse but rarely did they impugn his intelligence and quick mind.

As a Minister he did not relish piles of paper on his desk. He preferred action or a whispered plot or two, though he was already hard of hearing. He could be impulsive, as he showed when driving a car. Five years after his first wife died, he married Miss Mary Campbell at Christ Church in South Yarra, and that afternoon he took her for a honeymoon drive. On a deserted country road he flipped the car.

Hughes emerged as a natural leader of the Australian Labor Party at a time when it seemed to hold the nation's future in its hands. Upon Andrew Fisher stepping down as Prime Minister in October 1915, in the second year of the war, Hughes was elected unanimously as leader. He made an early visit to England and the battlefields on the western front, and captivated Britain with his arm-waving oratory. He also captivated his party's left-wing by buying 15 cargo ships for the new Commonwealth Shipping Line. He came home and promptly cut his party in two, splitting it almost with the blow of an axe.

He had been adamant that Australia should send more reinforcements to its existing volunteer army in France. The only sure way now was to conscript young men, train them and send them abroad. But the Labor

Party insisted that Australia's army - unlike most other wartime armies - should not be conscripted.

On this passionate question the nation itself was almost equally divided. Hughes had no intention of healing the division. In November 1916, he walked out of the Labor caucus - his expulsion was imminent - and took one-third of the members with him. Joining his forces with the Liberal opposition he remained Prime Minister.

The changeover was like the Canberra crisis of 1975 in its emotional impact. On both sides the rage was maintained. Hughes called a Federal election for May 1917 to endorse his stand. For his own political safety he had to move interstate, leaving his old seat of West Sydney and wisely contesting the more marginal Labor seat of Bendigo. His "Win the War" Nationalist Party decisively won the election; but he could not persuade the voters, at a later referendum, that they should support the compulsory recruiting of Australians for overseas battlefields.

Nor could he persuade most members of his new and conservative party that he was really "one of them". He remained in some ways a Labor man, expressing the kind of Australian nationalism which Labor had come to personify.

This was the complicated, unpredictable, powerful politician who was ready - as soon as the war ended - to tackle the Great Powers of the world with the same fearlessness which he employed against his own recalcitrant party in the Australian Parliament.

Hughes was determined, when the final peace treaty was negotiated in Europe, to snatch major concessions. He demanded that as many as possible of German's former island colonies in the west Pacific - and especially German New Guinea - be placed firmly under Australian control. Indeed, he would have liked to govern all the German islands in the West Pacific but he knew that Japan would successfully claim the Marshall Islands and those other German islands which its own forces had captured early in the war.

He also wanted Australia to receive from Germany a large sum in part-compensation for the 60,000 Australian lives lost in the war, for the huge debts incurred in financing that war, and maybe for the sums needed after the war to care for permanently disabled soldiers returning to Australia. He was to make yet another demand, with momentous implications for the world, after the peace negotiations began in France.

As Prime Minister, Hughes set out in April 1918 to attend meetings of the high-level Imperial War Council of which he was a member. He did not know when the war would end, and could not be certain that it would end that year. While he felt that the Germans would be defeated, even that hope was not completely assured. The fighting on the western front in Europe was still in deadlock, while on the eastern front Germany had decisively won, after revolutionist Russia retired.

The United States was belatedly in the war, and President Woodrow Wilson would clearly have a large say in the victory terms eventually imposed on Germany; and so Hughes hoped to meet him on his way to London. Sailing across the Pacific with his tiny entourage - but taking his own physician, for he suffered from dyspepsia - Hughes crossed the USA by train and met President Wilson in the White House where he put forward his views in his most disarming and moderate manner.

Hughes's resolve was that Australia should gain complete control of the old German New Guinea. For his part the President quietly hoped that Japan would never control those ex-German islands that might eventually serve as naval and submarine bases, not far from the route between San Francisco and the American Philippines.

In New York, Hughes won friends at a dinner put on by the Pilgrims Society. He emphasised that the question of which nation or international agency controlled such captured German colonies as Nauru and northern New Guinea was "of life and death importance to Australia". For an unfriendly power to control them was almost as if an enemy of England controlled the French port of Calais, just across the channel. Having shown the President his capacity for restraint, he was now showing the public his capacity for exaggeration.

The President and the Prime Minister were already far, far apart on the key issue. Wilson abhorred the punitive and crippling peace terms which Hughes wished to impose on Germany and which "Tiger" Clemenceau of France equally craved.

Wilson publicised his views in a benign memorandum known as the "14 Points", which the wily Clemenceau would later contrast with Christ's 10 Commandments. "Fourteen?" cried Clemenceau, "The Good Lord has only 10!"

For the time being, Wilson held the upper hand. His 14 Points were paraded as the formula and the bait with which to attract Germany into throwing down its arms. When at last, in November 1918, Germany suddenly collapsed, more from unrest in Berlin than from defeat on the battlefronts, it signed a firm armistice on the assumption that Wilson's 14 Points were likely to prevail when the victors decided upon precise terms of peace.

Hughes was in England on the day the armistice was signed. Dismayed when he heard of Wilson's backroom victory and Britain's quiet part in that victory, he did not retreat. He prepared to go to the peace negotiations in Paris in the new year not only as a leading member of the British Empire's delegation but loudly representing Australia in its own right as a victorious nation.

The other Australian delegate was Joseph Cook who was Hughes' right-wing partner in the new Parliamentary Coalition: Cook's humbler role in Paris was to take part in the creating of Czechoslovakia. In their personalities and politics the two leaders were far apart, but they had much in common. Cook had been a coal miner in England and had emigrated like Hughes in the mid-1880s. Both had grown up on the nonconformist fringes, Hughes' father belonging to the sect known as Particular Baptists, while Cook was a strong Primitive Methodist.

Both had been inspired when young by Henry George's idea of imposing what we would now call a massive capital-gains tax on land, and both were enticed to the new Australian Labor Party. Both dramatically parted company from Labor, with Cook departing when he was leader of the infant Parliamentary Labor Party in NSW and justifying his decision in retrospect by rising to become the Liberal Prime Minister in 1913. But most unusual of all was the sight of these two politicians - Hughes more than Cook - prepared to go to battle against the nation in which they had grown up.

In the emotion-charged negotiations that were to drag on until June 1919, when finally the German leaders signed the treaty, Hughes seemed likely to be a minor player. The Big Four stood dominant - Wilson of the USA, Lloyd George of Britain, Clemenceau of France, and Orlando of Italy. And below them were numerous nations which, counting their war dead, could outbid Hughes whenever he said proudly that he spoke on behalf of 60,000 Australians who were now lying silent on foreign soil.

And yet there were times when Hughes, by persistence and a sense of publicity, became a major player. He openly clashed with President Wilson - he sarcastically called him "The Great One" - on major issues. He did not back up Lloyd George's sensible plea that Germany be saved from humiliation.

No Australian politician has made such a mark for so long on the global stage as Hughes made in the first half of 1919. Ultimately he was to confess privately that he was disappointed at what he achieved: "It is _not_ a good peace for Australia." Of course he exaggerated. Australia won a mandate to govern German New Guinea, a right to financial reparations from Germany, and a remarkable victory on a disputed principle which became crucial both for Australia and Japan as the debates in Paris continued.

The Japanese delegation at the conference wished to insert in the covenant of the new League of Nations (the mother of the present UN) a statement affirming racial equality. Japan's desire was understandable. Even Hughes was not unsympathetic - so long as the covenant carried the distinct proviso that Australia and Japan and every other government could control its own immigration policy.

Deadlock soon ensued. Hughes fought for his view, punching as only he could punch. In the end the Japanese principle, though backed by a majority, was not added to the covenant. As one British observer said of

Hughes: "This strange man had the knack, possessed by none other, of knocking the President completely off his balance."

President Wilson was not the only leader who resented the fact that Australia, with a mere five million people, could several times deliver an ultimatum to a conference at which 1200 million people and a host of nations were represented. And yet Wilson probably felt a tinge more sympathetic to Hughes's attitudes than he dared to admit. Indeed, public opinion in the USA, at times, was more in tune with Hughes than with its own President.

Billy Hughes' contest with the Japanese in 1919 is now easily misunderstood - so far have those times and his values receded. Internationalism is now somewhat ascendant, especially in speech-making; and many influential Australians today would disown Hughes's conduct towards the Germans and the Japanese.

But if Hughes were to magically reappear in order to defend himself, he would presumably argue that the world was utterly different then, that he owed a duty to all Australians who had died for their country, and that his prime task was the strengthening of Australia's security in a vast but perilous ocean. Indeed if an unfriendly or neutral power had happened to hold such PNG ports as Rabaul early in the Second World War, then Japan might have quickly cut off the Australian continent.

Hughes proved himself a shrewder politician than Wilson who, on returning to America, failed to sell the treaty to his Senate. In contrast, Hughes sailed home to Fremantle, made his triumphant way in the new train across the Nullabor, and forcefully sold the treaty to the Australian Parliament.

He was to remain a politician until his death in Sydney in 1952, the only sitting survivor of that first national Parliament, and a law unto himself. In his last month, this stooped and shrunken man reached the age of 90 but insisted that he was only 88.

If this country becomes a republic, a host of Australians will for the first time argue that they are now independent in the eyes of the wider world.

But long ago an Australian Prime Minister was proclaiming to the great powers, assembled in Paris, an independence which was so persistent that nothing comparable is likely to be seen, either in a monarchical or a republican Australia, during the first half of the coming century.

A Sad Footnote

On the day the war ended only half of the victory had been won. The enemy, after four years of the most intense fighting in the history of the world, had been defeated. To the astonishment and dismay of most observers, the task of creating an effective peace treaty and reshaping the world proved itself more difficult than actually winning the war. What was won in 1914-18 was virtually lost in 1919.

The Age, 10 November, 1998

The Final Months of War

At the start of 1945 nobody in Australia could be sure when the war would end. Hitler's empire was still the largest Europe had seen since the days of Napoleon. Cities such as Hong Kong and Singapore, Djakarta and Saigon, and dozens of others were still in Japanese hands.

Almost 150,000 Japanese soldiers were in northern New Guinea and its adjacent islands. Against them were pitted Australian forces that were more numerous than those which, earlier in the war, fought in North Africa and Malaysia combined.

Australia's foremost soldier, General Sir Thomas Blamey, thought that the war might go on for 18 months. His private fear was that Australia might be excluded from the final assault on Java, the Malay peninsula, the Philippines, Hong Kong and Japan itself. His fear proved correct.

The American forces were commanded by the talented General McArthur whose ego - some critics implied - was bigger than Ayers Rock. He was determined that the pain and the final glory of conquering Japan would belong to him and to his huge American forces.

While American forces invaded the Philippines, the Australians were confined to "the backyard" of the near north in 1945. During this last phase of the war the Australian losses were heavy on Bougainville and on the north coast of the island of New Guinea. There, around Aitape and Wewak, Japan's losses were far heavier, some 14,000 dying through disease alone.

In May 1945, Australian soldiers, sailors and aircrew were allowed to take one step closer to the forefront of General MacArthur's stage. In the hope of capturing the east coast of Japanese-held Borneo with its strategic oilfields, they landed at Tarakan on 1 May, 1945. In a later landing at Balikpapan, 229 were killed.

Australia now was more important to the American war effort as a supply base and arsenal than as a source of fighting forces. To ease the shortage of labour in factories and farms, Australia had begun to demobilise long before the war was over. In the last two years of the war the army was reduced by 100,000 men.

The industrialising of the nation proved to be one of the mighty achievements of the war. By 1945 Australia was - by world standards - more important and versatile in manufacturing than it is today. Significantly, Port Melbourne was making sophisticated military aircraft years before it turned out the Holden car.

The defeat of Germany in May 1945 and the potential release of Allied arms for the campaigns in the Pacific was almost the final blow to Japan. But Japan did not accept defeat.

The island of Iwo Jima, a mere rock in the North Pacific, was a sign of Japanese grit. Held by a garrison of 22,000 Japanese, it was "softened up" by the heaviest bombing carried out by America in the whole Pacific War.

Then on 22 February 1945 it was invaded by 30,000 American marines. The Japanese defended until almost their last able-bodied man was dead. On that island alone the Japanese suffered a death roll two-thirds as large as that suffered by Australia in the entire war.

No wonder that thousands of Australian soldiers fighting in the tropics thought that the war "would go on for years". Even in the last week of the war, Japanese forces were safely entrenched close to the Australian continent. From such northern airfields as Darwin and Cairns, it was only a short flight to regions occupied by the Japanese.

Many Australians, as war-prisoners of the Japanese, were still tortured or beaten in the last days of the war. They had reason to fear that they would be executed by their Japanese guards, on the eve of liberation. Ossie Rudolph, a prisoner of the Japanese in Changi, recently recorded how his mates believed that "the Japs had specific orders to liquidate all POWs in Changi, in the event of a seaborne attack on Singapore or Malaya".

So far as we know, no high officials in Australia in August 1945 knew that the Americans, having manufactured atomic bombs, were about to drop them on two Japanese cities. If by chance Australians did know, they would have applauded the decision - terrible as the consequences would be for the people of Hiroshima and Nagasaki.

Japan was a fierce and often ruthless opponent. That is why its defeat, 50 years ago, should be celebrated far more than the bombing of Hiroshima and Nagasaki should be mourned.

Herald Sun, 14 August, 1995

IN OUR TIME

1945: The Long Awaited Year

On 15 August, 1945, the day when the war ended, Australians were jubilant. But a month later they were more wary. In conversations around the teapot on the kitchen table, there was not often a glowing optimism about the future.

The new era of the atom bomb was expected to be unsafe. Many Australians also predicted that unemployment would return just as it returned after the first world war. And yet many others, both left and right, believed that with determination and purpose they might somehow create a better Australia or what they called "a new order". In the Federal Parliament a white paper on full employment, introduced by J.J. Dedman as Minister for Post-war Reconstruction, even began with the moving words of Blake's *Jerusalem*.

Joseph Benedict Chifley, the nation's leader since John Curtin's recent death, was probably closer to socialism than any other Prime Minister in Australia's history. A steam-locomotive driver for much of his working life, he had educated himself in nearly everything from public finance to literature after he left school in Bathurst, and now in his 60th year his chance had come. In Canberra he and his colleagues sketched plans for providing more social security and economic regulation than Australians had ever known.

"Ben" Chifley believed in big government. Whereas privatising is now the vogue, Chifley wanted the opposite. To nationalise all interstate airlines and all the private banks was his hope. He was even to toy, about 1948, with a scheme for nationalising all private radio stations in Australia.

Politics was veering to the left, and Chifley puffed at his pipe with pleasure when he saw the first post-war illustration of the mood. An election was to be held for the late John Curtin's seat of Fremantle on 18 August, 1945, and commentators wondered what would happen, for it was a swinging seat. Indeed, on the Monday morning after the Federal election of 1940, John Curtin, then leader of the Labor Party, had been so far behind that he was thought to be defeated.

In 1945, Labor's victory in Fremantle was sweeping. Kim Beazley, the father of the present Deputy Prime Minister, won 57 per cent of the votes and Patrick Troy, the Communist, won another three per cent, leaving the Liberal candidate with a humiliating 33 per cent. The numerous ballot papers coming from the armed forces had been counted separately, and to the delight of Chifley, only one in every five of the forces' votes went to the Liberal.

It was in this leftist mood that Menzies formed his new political party. That he called it Liberal - though the Liberals in England stood to the left of Menzies - showed that he understood the post-war mood. Visiting Americans were puzzled that a conservative party should call itself Liberal but Menzies sensed that most post-war voters wanted regulation, if not carried to extremes.

The political divisions were deep in 1945 but sometimes a quiet generosity was noticed in each of the opposing leaders. Thus when Chifley, tired with work and strain, vanished from the headlines at Christmas 1945, his supporters hoped he had gone to rest in his cottage home in Bathurst; but instead he flew to New Guinea and Bougainville to spend time with thousands of troops still awaiting their turn to come home.

In the same year, Menzies, leader of the opposition, showed a spirit rarely felt in Federal Parliament today. Chifley had just been appointed a Privy Councillor, perhaps the highest honour a Labor man would accept in those days; and at question time Menzies made the most charming of short speeches - disguised as a question - in which he vowed that every member of every party "experiences the greatest possible personal pleasure" in the honour conferred on Chifley.

In the following four years, Chifley controlled daily life far more than most Australian people would now accept, but in 1945 they gladly accepted regulations in the belief that they were temporary and in the nation's interest in a time of scarcity and transition.

For a time Canberra's regulations were so like an octopus that not even an encyclopaedic politician knew them all: regulation of rents, regulation of food prices, regulation of the size and design of new houses, regulating of travel, regulating of the workplace of dentists as well as unskilled workers. Even the BHP shares were not allowed to rise beyond a certain price on the stock exchanges.

Various goods were still rationed. People had to hand in a rationing coupon to buy meat and sugar, butter and tea. Petrol was rationed until 1950. Many returning soldiers who were met at a country railway station noticed a tiny trailer behind the family car. This was the gas-producer which, filled with charcoal from a heavy bag, generated gas that drove the car. Occasionally falling cinders set alight the dry grass along the road.

It was not easy to buy a secondhand Ford, Chev, Dodge, Essex, Overland, Rugby or indeed any make. The chance of buying a new car was tiny. Tens of thousands of cars on the roads were models of the 1920s, many with soft hoods, cellophane windows, wide running-boards that carried the luggage, and tail lights that could only be turned on by the driver jumping down and striding to the back of the car and turning on the manual switch. Many people motoring at night put a woollen rug around their legs to keep out the cold breeze.

Nearly all other kinds of communciations were still impeded by wartime shortages. In 1942 the sending of congratulatory telegrams for Christmas, New Year and Mothers Day had been banned, and they did not appear again until the first Christmas after the war. In those days a telegram was delivered by a boy on a government bicycle.

At that time most houses in Australia possessed no telephone and almost half of the houses that did own phones still had to use a manual telephone exchange. You did not dial a number - rather you took the phone off the hook and waited for someone at the telephone exchange to pick up your call and dial the number you requested. In the country towns the "exchange girls", if time was heavy on their hands, listened to the conversation between callers. They could almost be heard breathing with excitement if the chatter flowing along the wires was gripping.

The idea of making an overseas phone call just did not enter most people's heads. The typical family, whether in Port Adelaide or Potts Point, had never made an overseas call and knew nobody who had.

For a year or two after the war, many goods were too scarce to be rationed and were rarely to be found. Beer, cigarettes and ready-rubbed tobacco were often in short supply. Cream, except in the country, was not easily found. A thousand items available in shops in 1940 could not be bought at the end of 1945.

Early in the war tens of thousands of Australians had predicted shortages and put away a small hoard of items likely to become unprocureable: imported tins of salmon and sardines, bottles of Scotch and imported lime juice and perfume, and 20 other kinds of foods and trinkets. Even when the war ended, many people kept their hoard untouched because the scarcity continued. By then some of the tins of food had gone bad and some had burst.

Australia then had only seven million people. Western Australia and Queensland were less important than they are today, and Perth was the kind of town where people walked along St Georges Terrace knowing they would run by chance into somone they knew.

Canberra was not yet amongst the big inland cities, being dwarfed even by Kalgoorlie. Darwin, once most of the service people had gone home, reverted to a sleepy town. The whole Northern Territory probably held fewer people than Bendigo.

Rural Australia had a strong voice. Nine of every 10 farming regions had more people then than now, and at hundreds of lonely crossroads stood church and school and maybe general store and post office that have since vanished or fallen into neglect. The farming and small-town vote was so large that no political party could hope to win a Federal election without earning some popularity in the countryside. In Victoria, the most industrialised state, the Country Party led by farmer Albert Dunstan was in its 10th year in office; and in most years it ruled with Labor and not Liberal support.

Farmers, then as now, were struggling. The typical farm was in debt, either to banks or to country storekeepers, many of whom were themselves in debt. To make matters worse, the rabbits were esconsed, for ever it seemed. In a lush year they seemed to own Australia. In 1949 the myxomatosis would begin to slaughter them.

We complain about droughts but in the south-eastern quarter of the continent a typical inland farmer and his wife aged about 50 had experienced more droughts and more dust storms than their children and grandchildren were to experience. Drought parched most wheatlands in the last phase of the war, and the red inland dust was carried by the wind to the south island of New Zealand where it thinly coated the snow.

The Victorian Mallee, Broken Hill and far-western towns were blinded by dust storms. In November 1944 some trains were halted by sands drifting on to the tracks, irrigation channels were filled by sand instead of water, and a frightened citizen of Mildura told the local paper that the end of the world must be in sight. Even if the wheat had been grown in abundance much of it would have been unsold, for overseas cargo ships had vanished. Western Australian wheat farmers were compelled by law to sow a far lower acreage.

To travel in 1945 from a city to a typical farm was to re-enter the 19th century. There was no electric light and no refrigerator. On a few thousand farms the heavy horses were still used for ploughing though the scarcity of labour was so acute that many farmers turned to tractors - if they could buy one. On Australian farms the wives were renowned for their hard work but in the war most worked even harder.

Even in the cities in 1945 the typical house did not have many labour-saving amenities. The most common were the electric iron, the ice chest, and the Singer sewing machine that was driven usually by foot.

Most houses did not own a washing machine. Mum was the washing machine, and the spin-dryer was the wind out of doors. Anyone who walked along a back lane in a suburb on Monday morning could hear the flapping sound coming from the wet washing that was pegged on the clothes lines in nearby backyards. Passers-by could also smell the wood smoke rising from the wash-house copper where the next batches of clothes were being boiled.

Television did not exist. The radio was triumphant and a radio star probably had as much fame as a TV star today.

The transistor radio and the car radio had not yet been invented. If you wanted to hear the radio in the open air, you opened the kitchen window and turned the volume up so you could do the gardening while listening to the magic horse Bernborough win his latest race.

Crowds would attend a radio studio if invited to form an audience. Occasionally, children were coaxed into speaking a sentence on "the wireless". After being escorted to the microphone, a child always sent a "big cheerio to mum, dad, Harry, Daphne, and all those listening in".

Alas, the cheerios that once filled the wartime airwaves have almost vanished, along with *First Light Fraser, The Village Glee Club, Dad and Dave, Big Sister, The Argonauts, The Search for the Golden Boomerang, The Australian Amateur Hour, Lux Radio Theatre*, and other specials which families looked forward to intensely and then talked about for days afterwards.

In the evening, while the radio was turned on, the ironing of shirts and dresses and the knitting, patching and mending of clothes was taking place. In those days, holes appeared frequently in the toes and heels of socks, and the women of the house darned them with needle and wool. The plastic socks and the drip-dry synthetic shirt belonged to the future.

Mornings for most people began by opening the newspaper. The Australian cartoon, more nationalist than ever, was enormously influential. Ginger Meggs, Bluey and Curly, Wally and the Major, Bill Bowyang, and other Australian comic characters saw the world with distinctive eyes.

No public relations venture by the army could efface the impression of military life that came from those raggle-taggle soldiers, Bluey and Curly.

It is in one of Alex Gurney's comic strips that a new soldier arrives at a jungle camp and greets Bluey and Curly, who in the cartoons always seem to be sitting around, smoking and yarning. "What," the new soldier asks, "are the mosquitoes like up here, sport?"

Bluey, his army hat askew, a cigarette dangling on his lip, replies bluntly, "Crook!". He casually adds that only the other night a "mob of mozzies came over and fair dinkum, they swooped down and carried off a tent and sewing machine".

Criticisms can easily be made of the way of life of 1945, but in some ways it was inferior and in some ways superior to today's. A capacity to laugh was one of its merits. To raise a laugh was a major occupation. The yarn-spinners and the tellers of jokes and tall stories must have numbered almost a million.

There was justifiably a pride in what Australia could do, and a deep satisfaction in its manufacturing achievements during the war years. Australia industrially was more self-sufficient than it is today. A visitor arriving by train in Newcastle for the first time felt the same delight in seeing the billowing smokestacks of BHP that a young Australian today might well feel at their absence.

Even in the front and back gardens of suburbia, nationalism was sprouting. Listen to "Waratah", the Sydney gardening expert, praising such Australian roses as Sunny South, Lorraine Lee, Warawee, Kitty Kininmonth and Salmon Spray: "Our home raised roses are like their country of birth - strong, free and bright - with typical Australian characteristics, healthy and vigorous." The pride, slightly overstated, was felt widely in city and bush.

Eating habits had little changed in the last 40 years. A city restaurant or café was a rarity partly because most people had no money to spare on such luxuries. On the other hand, some of today's luxuries were cheap. In Tasmanian towns the scallops and mutton birds were cheap pleasures in season. Crayfish were not yet exorbitant in price, and a labourer on his way home from the pub on Saturday night might halt at the fish and chip shop to buy a large crayfish wrapped in newspaper.

A big meal at midday was still common, especially in the country towns. It was often called "dinner". The evening meal was nothing without a pudding. Today the restaurant pages of magazines tend to sneer at oldtime Australian cooking, and certainly it could be stodgy. But it starred with the cakes and puddings that have now slipped from fashion: Yorkshire pudding and lemon sauce, plum pudding, treacle pudding, tapioca pudding, sliced bananas in hot custard. An able cook, short of an ingredient, turned to the Golden Syrup tin, known widely as the "cocky's delight".

Nurses and airmen back from the war were often reassured to see familiar sights: the bread always placed on the wooden breadboard and cut into slices by the head of the household who rightly sat at the head of the table. Packaged food was still uncommon. The packet of sliced bread was probably unknown in Australia.

The idea of a self-service supermarket was unimaginable. In a big city like Sydney, nine of every 10 families lived in walking distance of a grocer's shop. The grocer himself, with his white apron and lead pencil behind his ear, was the packager. Much of his time was spent behind the fortress-like counter, filling and weighing brown-paper bags of sugar, flour, salt, wholemeal for the porridge, or bags of biscuits taken by hand from the big tin.

A grocer might have a boy to help him. Grocer's and butcher's boys soon learned how to take a few running steps and slide on their feet along the sawdust floor, like skaters on ice.

Social taboos remained strong, and gambling was virtually prohibited except on the racecourses, and the drinking of alcohol was discouraged by the closing of hotels in Victoria and South Australia at six o'clock and by the shortage of bottled beer. Wine was looked down upon. A wine saloon was really the home of the tuppeny dark and other cheap fortified wines.

Old practices and penalties were still applied in many facets of life and death. In 1946 in both Tasmania and South Australia one criminal was hanged. Education, like the criminal law, changed slowly; and most girls and boys left school after grade eight and entered the workforce. Nonetheless, education had prestige: teachers possibly were held in slightly higher esteem then than now.

Divorce was frowned upon: in the whole nation in a typical week there were only 50 or 60 divorces. Couples were usually married in a church, on a Saturday afternoon, and at their wedding reception the chance was probably 40-60 that no alcohol would be served. A typical marriage involved people of the same religion, and most Presbyterians married Presbyterians and nearly all Catholics married Catholics.

A honeymoon in 1945 was almost invariably spent at a nearby resort or city. To travel more than 100 miles away for a honeymoon was an adventure and a half.

The idea of flying away for a honeymoon was inconceivable, for aircraft tickets were expensive and civilian passengers were unlikely to be allotted a seat. When they did manage to wangle a seat they were likely to be offloaded at the last moment if an important politican, officer or bureaucrat decided to travel.

To travel overseas by aircraft was an ordeal but a thrill. Australia's best known scientist, Sir David Rivett, decided in 1946 to make his first foreign visit for nearly a decade. At Mascot he boarded a noisy four engine Lancastrian with seats for nine and was delighted - after leaving the north Australian coast - to look down on so many rivers and villages in the Dutch East Indies and British India, for the plane cruised at a low height at only 200 miles an hour.

To London, with various stops for fuel, was a journey of only four days and three nights. Most people who went to Britain spent about a month at sea.

For several hundred thousand Australians back from the war, the excitement of 1945 was finding and keeping a job. Unemployment, close to 10 per cent on the eve of war, was almost down to 1 per cent. It would have been even lower but for the industrial disputes which, centred in New South Wales, cost two million working days in 1945.

Everywhere was a yearning for the return of big-time sport. International contests, abandoned since 1939, were awaited eagerly by sport-starved fans. The last Test Cricket match had been played at The Oval in

August 1938 when England won by an innings and 579 runs and Len Hutton made the staggering score of 364.

When would England tour Australia? That burning topic was discussed even by the prisoners of war as they returned home from east Asia.

At last the English cricketers arrived by ocean liner late in 1946 and went to Brisbane for the match that several million Australians had been longing for. When Don Bradman walked out to the wicket, every second Australian ear was glued to the radio. He made 187 but poor Len Hutton was dismissed twice by dashing Keith Miller for a humble total of seven. To many Australians, nothing else signified so magically the coming of peace.

The ordinary players of games had to wait a while for the return of peacetime equipment. Many tennis balls were hit on court until they were bald, chipped golf balls were used, and in the playground of schools the children kicked footballs made of newspaper tightly rolled.

It was a wonderful era for words and nicknames. In 1945 Sidney Baker produced the best book so far written on Australia's own words and phrases, and he listed a host of words coined mostly in Australia during the war and now widely used. The return of servicemen and servicewomen gave "army slang" a wider popularity. Conscripts and militiamen were chocos. A loafer was a spine basher or a bludger. A mess was a balls-up; and an idiot or nitwit was a drongo or a galah. To boast or to talk too assertively was to shoot one's head off.

In the aftermath of war the nation was not inclined to shoot its head off. The future was a puzzle. Nothing could be more contrasting than the optimism after the First World War - the war to end all wars - and the cagey caution of 1945.

The soldiers returning from France in 1919 and expecting much of the world were to be shabbily treated: they entered a world of high unemployment with another world war 20 years later. But the soldiers, nurses, sailors and airmen returning home in 1945-46 did not expect too much and were doubly rewarded with an era of full employment lasting perhaps a quarter of a century and a freedom from world wars which has now lasted half a century.

The Australian Magazine, 19-20 August, 1995

IN OUR TIME

Australia and Air Power

Even before the outbreak of the First World War there were glimpses of how aircraft would be used in warfare, but nobody could foresee the sheer magnitude of their power. The Italians were the first to use aircraft in war. Fighting the Turks in North Africa in 1911 and 1912 their aeroplanes mapped the movements of the enemy and even attacked them: most aerial attacks depended on the firing of rifles and even of revolvers from the aircraft.

In 1914, in the opening months of the First World War, aircraft were used to spy on the enemy army far below. As the Germans swept through Belgium and north-east France in that remarkable sweeping movement, British aircraft observed the danger to General French's army. Their pilots, however, did not photograph what they saw. The planes could not easily carry the heavy cameras of that era.

In some military aircraft the propeller was at the rear, thus enabling an airman to shoot at the target he could see in front of him - without damaging the propeller. In May 1915, the Germans took the enemy by surprise when their Fokker aircraft were able to fire through the propeller.

At first the Germans thought that their massive airships flying at 25 to 40 miles an hour and dropping their bombs from on high would destroy the morale of British civilians. Their raids were infrequent but frightening. In the course of the war German air raids on English cities were to kill 1413 people. The French, after Paris was bombed, retaliated with raids on German cities - Cologne and Stuttgart were targets. On Christmas Eve 1917, a British squadron dropped a ton of bombs on the German city of Mannheim. What a devastating show of force, said some observers.

Both the big airships and frail aeroplanes became important in the search for submarines in near-coastal waters or in detecting enemy warships. Aircraft were vital in informing the artillery on the success or failure of their bombardments. Occasionally aircraft attacked troops with success. In Palestine in 1918 the Turkish 7th Army was trapped in a ravine and bombed, with heavy casualties.

The aircraft carrier appeared: at first an orthodox ship lowering onto the calm water a little seaplane which then climbed into the sky. The fixed position of the mast and funnel on warships made it slightly difficult to build an airfield on a ship's deck, but it was accomplished. Planes found it easier to take off than to land. In order to facilitate their return the British built in the large warship *Furious* a special landing deck at the opposite end to the take-off deck. The eddies of wind around the funnel and the effect of the smoke belching out still made a landing difficult. By 1925 the modern big aircraft carrier had arrived, and the United States had built two giants and Japan had built one giant, each of about 33,000 tons with a supposed speed of 33 knots.

By the end of the First World War the aircraft had become pervasive. In the Second World War they would be decisive.

The civilian aircraft were especially welcome in the Australian continent with its abundant landing strips, and its relative freedom from fog and cloud, and the lack of competing forms of transport in so many regions. QANTAS, the world's second-oldest airline, began in the dry interior of Australia, its tiny passenger planes hopping from small town to small town. The initials of QANTAS stand for Queensland and Northern Territory Aerial Services, a sign of its outback origins.

Australians, out of all proportion to their numbers, were enthusiasts for the new art of flying. Many learned to fly during the First World War. In 1919 two such airmen, Ross and Keith Smith, were the first to fly from Europe to Australia. Their adventure occupied 24 days. They had no radio and usually no weather forecasts of the route ahead; they usually flew in daylight, at 80 miles an hour.

Australians pioneered many of the world's long air routes. In the 1920s, Charles Kingsford-Smith and C.T.P. Ulm were the first to fly across the Pacific and the Tasman Sea. Wilkins made the first transpolar flight, flying from Alaska to Spitzbergen in 1928. Hinkler, from the sugar town of

Bundaberg, was the first to fly across the Atlantic from South America to Africa, a west-east flight. Several of these aviators died while attempting new records. Hinkler is buried just outside Florence in Italy. Kingsford-Smith has no grave.

In Australia the aircraft gave rise to a new, exciting form of sport. The air race occasionally rivalled the big horse race in glamour. Indeed, the air races often ended on the race courses near the heart of the main cities. Australia's first air race was in 1912, from Sydney to the outer suburb of Parramatta. W.E. Hart, flying a Bristol Box-kite, won in 23 minutes. His opponent, known as The Wizard, flew into a rain cloud and lost his way. In 1934 the most glamorous event when Victoria and Melbourne celebrated their centenary was an air race from London to Melbourne. Even airliners could compete in their own special section, and the Dutch KLM crossed the world in a Douglas C2 in the remarkable time of three days and 18 hours.

Australia's imagination was captured by aircraft. Our 20 dollar note reflects this absorption. On one side is the portrait of Hargrave, who about 100 years ago was conducting aeronautical experiments just south of Sydney: a man far ahead of his time, he was not in the mainstream of the development of aviation. On the other side of the 20 dollar note is Kingsford-Smith, a hero in what you might call the Stanley and Livingstone era of exploration by air.

The Australian people and traditions, enthusiastic about aircraft in times of peace, have been ambivalent towards aircraft in times of war. When Australians think of their nation's past wars they think firstly of the army and secondly of the navy. Nearly all the overseas wars to which Australia sent forces were primarily land wars - the war against New Zealand's Maoris in the 1860s, the Sudan war in the 1880s (the Australians, too far away, arrived too late), the Boer War fought between 1899 and 1902, the First World War. The Malayan insurgency, and the Korean and Vietnam Wars. In those wars most or all Australians were soldiers. In most of those wars Australian naval vessels were vital or useful.

What about attitudes to air power? In the Second World War, especially in the Pacific War (1941-45), air power was crucial for Australia's success but outside military and strategic circles its importance in that war has largely been forgotten. Of course many individuals - indeed everyone present here tonight - understands the influence of air power but Australians as a people do not remember the role of air power in the early 1940s when their own nation was endangered. Today their education system - if the word "system" can be used to describe benign chaos - largely ignores air power if and when it teaches students about the danger facing Australia during that war.

Today the most frequent recollection of the Pacific War centres on the Australian prisoners of war, and the cruelty and hardship which they experienced while working for the Japanese on the Burma railway and other projects. Australians understandably remember the cruelty. They fail to remember why some 20,000 Australians were captured after the fall of Singapore and the collapse of the Dutch East Indies. They were captured because the loss of sea power prevented them from retreating and from organising a "tropical Dunkirk". Control of the seas was lost because power in the air was lost.

In Australia's history the dominant military legend is the landing of Australian soldiers at Gallipoli on 25 April, 1915 and the bravery shown by the soldiers during their months on a narrow beach-head. There are strong reasons why the day of their invasion, Anzac Day, remains in Australia a day of remembrance. But it would be better for Australia's future security if the Fall of Singapore, 27 years later, were remembered with the same vividness.

It is unwise for Australian public opinion to attribute military success, and we do that when we remember Gallipoli, solely to such human virtues as self-sacrifice and perseverance and to forget the power of technology. The biggest difference between fighting the Turks at Gallipoli and the Japanese at Singapore was that Australians held the superior technology at Gallipoli and the inferior technology at Singapore. In 1942, air power was the key element in military technology. It is salutary to observe that if, at Gallipoli, the Turks and their German allies gained the same kind of air superiority or the same control of the lines of communications as the Japanese gained at Singapore, then Gallipoli probably would have been abandoned quickly by the Australians as well as the British, French, Indian and New Zealand forces there.

Woe betide the nation which misunderstands its own wartime history. If you were to ask well-informed Australians why Singapore was conquered in 1942, most would give a definite naval answer, not an air answer. They would say with some scorn or puzzlement that in Fortress Singapore the artillery pointed out to sea when it should have pointed inland, towards Malaysia. In other words they maintain that the big mistake, before the outbreak of war, was that the British fortified Singapore in expectation of a naval attack from the enemy. There is some validity in such an explanation but it misses the main point. It would not have mattered where Singapore's big guns pointed. Japanese air power, more than its army, defeated the British and Australian forces, if I read my history correctly.

In Australian eyes, the other vital military episode of the Pacific War was fought three months after the Fall of Singapore. The Japanese, having captured Rabaul from the Australians, resolved to push south and capture Port Moresby from the sea. Part of the Japanese naval force was intercepted in the Coral Sea - in effect a vast gulf fronted by Queensland and New Guinea. In that tropical sea, on 7 and 8 May, 1942, the opposing American and Japanese fleets, completely out of sight of each other, fought a crucial battle that proved to be the first major repulse to the Japanese in the war.

Partly because it is called the Battle of the Coral Sea, it is seen by most educated Australians as a naval battle. Indeed many books on Australian history interpret it simply as a battle between ships. And yet it was primarily fought by aircraft. The rival navies did not even fire on one another.

That vital battle was fought close to Australia. The American aircraft carrier *Lexington* was sunk a mere 600 miles from the Queensland coast. If the Japanese had won -rather than drawn - that battle, they would have probably driven the Australians and Americans from New Guinea, thus exposing Australia to great danger. The Australian people, as distinct from high officials, have never celebrated the anniversary of the Battle of the

Coral Sea. It is seen as too American a victory. No nation, in retrospect, likes to be rescued by its ally, though that is the very purpose of having an ally!

Air power, essential in those two dramatic events, the Fall of Singapore and the Battle of the Coral Sea, is given surprisingly little weight in Australian memory. Of course there are books which tell a more realistic story, and there are strategists and historians and returned servicemen who know what happened: but on the whole neither educated opinion nor public opinion knows about the role of air power in saving Australia from isolation and even possible invasion. In a democracy, public opinion is crucial in the long term. It helps to determine the nation's high priorities and the priority - if any - given to defence.

The importance of air power, in these episodes crucial to our nation's survival, has been largely forgotten by Australians. A nation's defence is too important to be afflicted by Alzheimer's.

I conclude with a word about the future. In my opinion there are, amongst independent nations, few cultures as vulnerable as Australia's to a major surprise in warfare. Sometime in the future we are likely to be surprised, either by the sudden outbreak of a war affecting us, or by a lightning strike that begins the war. We have become a complacent nation, a laid-back people. Complacency, unbelievable complacency, is a major cause of our economic decline. We are also, more than most other nations, likely to be surprised because we have a powerful sporting tradition of which the idea of fair play is part. We forget that in war the sporting rules do not necessarily apply.

Furthermore, we have a long tradition of relying on powerful allies, firstly Britain and now the United States. With our alliances we traditionally have been amongst the top dogs, and the top dog is less likely to use surprise as a weapon at the start of a war: the top dog has less need of that weapon. Surprise is the special instrument of the underdog. We have had little experience of being the underdog, and indeed have only once - in Vietnam - been on the losing side. We have never been the underdog for the duration of a war.

In the realm of surprises, we did not digest the lesson of Pearl Harbour. We are still inclined to think that the Japanese were especially treacherous, indeed abnormal, in attacking Hawaii and Malaysia and the Philippines without issuing a warning or declaration in December 1941. But wars again and again have commenced without a warning. A prior declaration of war, the issuing of a warning of attack, is unusual. When two opponents are separated by sea rather than a common land border, the sea provides a special opportunity for a surprise attack. The underdog will always be tempted to use that opportunity.

As Australians we tend to view military events more through the West European experiences. In Europe the typical war begins with an invasion by land, and such an attack can rarely be accompanied by a high level of surprise. In contrast Australia is surrounded by sea, and so an attacker or retaliator is likely to use surprise, partly because it is easier to employ surprise in crossing an air-sea gap and partly because it is necessary for the attacker to use surprise to compensate for the disadvantage which the sea barrier imposes.

I am not pointing a finger at any particular foreign power. The strained relationship, the issues of dispute, which precede a war may be as much the fault - or more so - of Australia than another nation. I am not being pessimistic. I am rather optimistic in the sense that I think that with effort Australia can overcome its vulnerability. Our vulnerability stems partly from a state of mind and therefore is changeable. Surprise succeeds only when one power is complacent. Surprise, to be successful, depends as much on the incompetence of the victim as the competence of the assailant.

Surprise is really a two-barrel rifle, and the victim, without knowing it, actually fires the second barrel. Our history, our culture, suggest that unless we wake up we could one day be a victim.

Address to the RAAF's 70th anniversary conference,
March 1991

IN OUR TIME

The Jews Flourished in Australia

The Jews form an astonishingly powerful group in Australia. They themselves rarely say so – or, if they do, they mainly say it in private. In proportion to their numbers, they surely are the great achievers in Australia in the past 100 years. You only need to examine the history of commerce, the law, medicine, most other professions and several of the arts, and Jewish names emerge in long, distinguished columns.

It could be argued that the Jews are influential rather than powerful. To say that they are powerful implies a unity of outlook, a common purpose which is not always there. Like any talented group of people they have their differences, and the story of Jews in Australia is the history of disputes among themselves at least as much as the history of disputes between Jews and Gentiles. But it is legitimate to suggest that in the past 40 years the Jews have been—in a way not possible 50 or 100 years ago—an unusually powerful people.

Their remarkable contribution to Australian life was a fact more widely known to earlier Australians than to those who are now aged between, say, 15 and 30. Somehow, somewhere, whether in TV programs or in school textbooks, there was diffused in recent years the Grassby-Pilger myth that Anglo-Celtic Australia trampled on all alien minorities. As an example of this view, a reporter recently phoned to say that she was writing a feature article about Jews in pre-war Melbourne, and she wished to have a historian's explanation of why Melbourne as a city had always been so "deeply hostile" to the Jews.

At first I could only blink. Of course there was prejudice against Jews but there was also respect: and without the respect the Jews of Melbourne, small in number, could not have provided more governors-general (ceremonially the highest office in the land) than did the local adherents of the largest religious group, the Anglicans. Without community respect, a Melbourne Jew could not have risen to become Australia's most famous soldier. In the past century and a quarter, there can be few cities in the world—Manchester may be another—and few other nations in the world where Jews, constituting such a minority, have earned so much distinction.

In some ways this is an easy decade for the public discussion of ethnic and racial differences within Australia: in other ways the topic is taboo. Despite the talk about the reign of multiculturalism, many real ethnic topics are—when the discussion comes down to tin tacks—too hot to handle. A cry of "discrimination" or "racism" often silences the discussion.

Fortunately two recent volumes, *The Jews in Australia*, break a vast extent of new ground. Written by Hilary and W.D. Rubinstein, they indirectly throw light on the question: why are Jews in so many ways successful when most Australians— as the state of the economy reveals—are not mighty contributors to the nation's economic competitiveness?

The history of Jews in Australia is not all hard work and economic success. Six Jewish convicts entered Sydney Harbour in the First Fleet in 1788. One, John Harris, transported for stealing eight silver table-spoons, was to be a direct ancestor of yet another governor-general, Lord Casey. About 1,000 Jewish convicts came to Australia, mostly thieves or pickpockets. There was no sign in those early decades that Jews would come to wield such influence in Australian life.

Before long, free Jewish settlers were landing to mingle with ex-convicts, and by the 1840s towns such as Sydney and Melbourne and Hobart had their synagogues, and they even showed special concern for the well-being of Jews living in Palestine, then under Turkish rule. In 1854, in response to the British chief rabbi's appeal for funds to help Jews and to launch farming and industrial projects in Palestine, one-third of his total contributions came from Australian Jews.

In Australian towns where one imagines there was never a Jewish presence, synagogues were built. Launceston in the late 1840s held about 450 Jews, although in the next quarter-century all but a few vanished, leaving only a Jewish cemetery, some 13 living adherents, and the Sefer Torah (the scroll of the five books of Moses) residing in such loneliness that it was carried to Hobart for safe-keeping. The concentration of Jews in

Melbourne and Sydney was not yet so visible, and synagogues with flourishing congregations could be found in inland towns. Toowoomba built the first synagogue in Queensland—later it passed into Lutheran hands—and even Coolgardie and Kalgoorlie had their synagogues, although slowly the members moved away or died, with Kalgoorlie in 1931 clutching at help by trying to affiliate with the liberal Beth Israel synagogue in Melbourne. Broken Hill had its Hebrew Minister as late as 1944. It was not the only big outback town with a synagogue as well as a mosque.

Anti-Semitism – a word which dates only from 1879 – was active at times in colonial Australia. The novelist Marcus Clarke expressed it strongly, especially in attacks on the Melbourne moneylender Aaron Waxman from whom Clarke borrowed heavily. Most of the anti-Semitism in Australia was specifically against the Jews as financiers and employers: in Hilary Rubinstein's phrase it was economic anti-Semitism. And yet she concludes that Jews generally met "undoubted tolerance and goodwill".

They won social equality through their ability and assertiveness and their willingness to assimilate while retaining their own Saturday as holy day. Jews became very prominent in the Freemasons (Phillip Blashki's jeweller's shop had the monopoly for supplying Masonic regalia in Australia), joined the nationalist Australian Natives Association, and won more than their share of seats in colonial Parliaments.

So eagerly did Jews throw in their lot with mainstream Australia that the synagogues' losses to other religions were large. Today in many towns such surnames as Cohen and Levy denote Protestantism— "the legacies of the lone and often lonely pedlars who hawked their wares through the outback and were tempted to stay there, intermarrying with Gentile women", or drifting away from their religion because the nearest synagogue was far away. The people who have a dash, large or small, of Jewish ancestry and retain no link with Judaism are probably three times as numerous as those who call themselves Jewish.

The rise of Zionism in Europe in the 1890s and the belief that there should be a special homeland for Jews did not halt the Australian Jews' tendency to absorb themselves in their adopted land. Such celebrated Jews as Sir John Monash and Sir Isaac Isaacs had mixed feelings about Zionism. Isaacs, while welcoming Palestine as a land for Jewish refugees, feared that it might win too emotional an attachment from young Jews and make them feel exiles so long as they remained on Australian soil.

The typical Jewish spokesman in the inter-war years, tactful and unassertive and of impeccable English speech, did not wish to rock the boat. Jewish parents and grandparents had worked so hard to become British-Australians that their children in the 1930s, understandably, were fearful of losing their hard-won ground by pleading for the entry of large numbers of Jewish refugees into Australia. But until 1941 the refugees poured in, increasing the Jewish population by one-third. The old Jewish Australian was about to be besieged.

The fate of Jews in Hitler's Europe, Australia's post-war switch in immigration policy and the emergence of the nation of Israel quickly transformed the Jewish peoples in Australia. The small Jewish population, enlarged by the influx of refugees from Hitler, was multiplied by half again in the years 1947 to 1952. Long an inward-looking people, Australian Jews now looked outwards. Israel competed with Australia for their loyalties. Above all, Australian Jews became important in a global picture. Sixty years ago Australian Jews ranked no higher than 40th on the numbers-ladder of world Jewry but today they rank 10th.

In Australian history there never has been an economic group as successful as the Jews of the past quarter-century. The Scots, kings of Australian counting houses and sheep runs a century ago, could not match this record. Admittedly in the years 1860-1900 the Scots had more prominence in the prestige posts of business and commerce than the Jews hold today; and certainly the McIlwaiths and McBains and their ilk held more power in the big public companies of a century ago than is held by Jews in, say, the top 100 public companies today—Jewish businessmen seem to thrive more in individual than corporate enterprises. But in proportion to population the Jewish role in business today makes the old-time Scots seem way down the field.

In some of the annual lists of the 200 wealthiest persons and families in Australia in the past decade, more than 50 are Jewish. As Professor W.D. Rubinstein comments: "The Jewish percentage here has been truly staggering—indeed embarrassing—and implies that Jewish talent has gone very disproportionately into business life during the past 30 or 40 years." For a long time there was little realisation among the general public or even sections of the business world that so many of the successful businessmen were Jewish. Names such as Sportsgirl and Katies have no Jewish sound, and many new entrepreneurs have surnames which to old Australian ears carry no Jewish echo.

Most of the New Rich came from central and eastern Europe: Larry Adler and Sir Peter Abeles from Hungary, the Blooms and Finks from Poland, Herscu from Romania and the Smorgon family from Russia. The old Jewish mercantile families of Australia are hardly to be found in the top 200. Nearly all the founders of these new fortunes stepped ashore after 1938, a fact which makes the Smorgons (class of 1926) seem like old pioneers.

Maybe half of these entrepreneurs are survivors of the Holocaust. Most were born between 1915 and 1940, and Poland and Hungary supplied the biggest number, with the Polish-Jewish millionaires living today in Melbourne and the Hungarians in Sydney. The acute despair experienced in wartime Europe and the desire to gain the maximum security in the new world must partly explain the astonishing drive and financial success of these men. True, they met mediocre competition from those native Australians who were dwelling serenely in a lotusland whose patron saint was "Sheelberight".

It is fair to say—on the basis of existing evidence—that these successful Jews mostly did little for our balance of payments. They were rarely to be seen in export industries and probably did less than the pre-war Jewish businessmen in the vital field of import-replacement. In favouring city property and in shunning those industries which had to compete with the outside world, the post-war Jewish promoters were like most other Australian investors.

One astonishing thing about Australian Jews is that, given the talent that goes into business, the overflow to other pursuits is in such volume. Their role in law, medicine and higher academic posts is eye-catching. W.D. Rubinstein estimates that in those professions the Jews have possibly five per cent of the places, or 10 times as many places as their share of the total Australian population would suggest.

In some fields revered by Australians, Jewish competitors are not conspicuous. For example the only two well-known Jewish cricketers are Julian Weiner and Ray Phillips who, although recent players, are probably not remembered by the average sports fan. It may be that in sport the Jews simply have the rate of success one would expect from a group holding only 0.5 per cent of the total population. But to say that Jewish Australians shun tough activities is an exaggeration. Their enlistment rate in the forces in the First World War was high.

Interestingly, since 1945 the direct Jewish role in politics has not been high. Only eight Jewish politicians have gone to Canberra in elections since 1945 and three of them have been Ministers. Seven of the eight were Labor members, a sharper ratio than the voting preference of Jews as a whole. It is likely that Jews tended to vote Labor in the 1950s but Liberal by the 1970s.

How they vote today is not known, although in some elections their vote must be partly coloured by the fact that Bob Hawke, more than any political leader in Australian history, has gone out of his way—sometimes with impressive courage—to take the Jewish side on international issues. On the other hand, he has pursued migration policies which have quickly built up the Islamic population.

On present indications the Australian Jews could well be near the peak of their remarkable influence. Another wave of Jewish immigration, like the 1936-55 wave, could maintain or even increase that influence, though it is unlikely that, say, 90,000 incoming Soviet Jews would have the same burning motivation to succeed as 30,000 immigrants of the Holocaust generation. Influence, however, depends not only on numbers but also on organising skill, dedication and money.

I see two potential limits to the continuing exercise of Jewish influence on foreign and national policies, as distinct from its influence on the professions, business and daily life. One limit is the growing muscle of Islam in Australia. Numerically Islamic lobbies far outnumber Jewish lobbies, and they probably will also increase their organising skills, though in electioneering funds they lag far behind. When more is discovered about the Labor Party's negotiations on the eve of recent Federal elections, we will almost certainly find that the Islamic lobby gained striking concessions in NSW. In short, the Jewish political influences, even on a Prime Minister as supportive as Hawke, are probably not as sweeping as they seem.

Another potential limit to the Jews' influence on Australia's national policy is their absorption in Israel and its problems. If they identify too closely with Israel, and if they are publicly believed to have too much success in shaping Australia's policy, there will be a reaction against such an influence. The pre-war Australian Jews and their pursuit of quiet assimilation are not viewed too kindly today by Jewish opinion-leaders, but in their own way the earlier men, the Monashes and Isaacs, patiently built up goodwill among the Australian public. In contrast, this generation of Jewish leaders, if they were to go too far in the opposite direction, would ultimately endanger the goodwill they now receive.

The Jews in Australia, if all lived in the one city, would merely fill a Ballarat or a Toowoomba. In a democracy, the continuing political power of such a tiny minority also depends, in the last analysis, on public consent.

Independent Monthly, November 1991

IN OUR TIME

Did the Forties Mould Australia?

The last 10 years are widely seen as the sharp turning point in Australia's history - a pointer to an Asian and global future far different from the past. But in Australia every modern decade thinks that it is *the* pathfinder.

Eventually it may transpire that the Hawke-Keating era was the dynamo of astonishing change but it is too early to tell. My conclusion is that so far the most influential decade is one that has almost slipped from the nation's memory - the 1940s.

Australia in 1940 would be viewed as a museum piece if 10-year olds could revisit it today. In 1940 it held only seven million people, and Sydney and Melbourne were less than half of their present size. In 1940 Canberra was a country town that pulled down its blinds before dark. A university degree was as uncommon as a refrigerator, a traffic jam was more likely to be found on a city footpath than on the road, and a family holiday spent 100 km from home was as exciting - and the occasion for more elaborate preparations - than a trip to Rome today. Of every 100 Australians, maybe 99 had not flown in an aeroplane. Of every 100 adults, maybe 60 did not touch alcohol more than once a year.

On 1 January, 1940 Australia was officially at war but nobody could confidently call it a World War. So far it was more a war centred on Poland. And yet in the next five years a prodigious war was fought, partly on Australia's front doorstep, and the nation was changed forever.

Even if Australia converts to a republic that event is not likely to have such an effect on Australian-British relations as a tragedy in the tropical seas on 10 December, 1941. At a time when Britain was believed by Australian observers to have the strongest navy in the world - a navy which was the front line of Australia's own defences - two mighty British warships, *Prince of Wales* and *Repulse*, were sunk near the coast of Malaysia by Japanese aircraft. Suddenly most Australians sensed how alone they were. The military and naval alliance which had been the core of Australian history for 150 years would never be the same.

Nearly every person over the age of 40 probably remembers where they themselves were on that day in 1963 when President Kennedy was assassinated; but how many over the age of 60 remember what they were doing on a more significant date, 8 December, 1941? That was the day when Japan attacked the American base at Pearl Harbour and began the chain of events which permanently altered Australia's alliances.

There was no ceremonial signing of the new Australian-American alliance. It just arose, out of sheer need and convenience. Admittedly it is feasible that the treaty Mr Keating signed with Indonesia during his last months in office will prove to be a diplomatic landmark in Australian history - a treaty which children one day will recite in school. But on present evidence it is unlikely to be as important as the treaty that was not signed in Washington or Canberra during the Australian summer of 1941-42.

On the eve of what became a strong and long-lasting alliance the diplomatic links between Australia and the United States were new. John Curtin, Australia's Prime Minister, made his celebrated appeal to the United States for military help, not in Parliament and not at a press conference but primarily in an impressive essay he wrote for the afternoon Melbourne *Herald*. Not a headline-seeking article, it began with a verse by the Melbourne poet Bernard O'Dowd... "That reddish veil which o'er the face / Of night-hag East is drawn..".

Curiously, by most measures the arts now possess more status in Australian life, and are more subsidised and talked about than they were half a century ago. But critics sometimes exaggerate the change in the relevance of the arts to national life. Which politician today, Federal or state, would imitate John Curtin and begin an epoch-making political statement with a quotation from a living, slightly highbrow Australian poet?

At the end of six years of war most Australians had learned hard lessons. One lesson they did not spell out loudly because it was - and is -

embarrassing. The Japanese pushed south with such ease in the first months of the Pacific War, and captured and imprisoned so many Australian servicemen, partly because public opinion in Australia had not been prepared for war and was not willing to equip the fighting forces adequately. Even after the war began in Europe, some of its leaders hoped that the war could be pushed out of sight.

We learn a lot by comparing the landing at Gallipoli in the first war and the collapse of Singapore in the second war. Whereas at Gallipoli the Australians, New Zealanders, British and French held the superior equipment and also secure lines of supply, Australia and its allies lacked these advantages in Malaysia and Singapore. Thus a successful evacuation from Gallipoli was organised at the end of 1915. Indeed it was more triumphant than the landing on 25 April because no Australian was killed. But there was no calm retreat from Singapore and Java. The Japanese commanded both air and sea and so captured an army of Australians, thousands of whom were to die in their camps.

From six years of war, and from the knowledge that defeat had been narrowly averted, most Australians resolved that the nation must become stronger in order to face a foreign threat - should it arise again. This determination shaped the following quarter century. There was a massive attempt to make Australia self-sufficient. Eventually factories employed - not always efficiently - close to one-third of the workforce, making Australia a far more significant manufacturing nation than it is today.

The Second World War inspired a popular demand to build up population so that if Australia was again imperilled it could resist an invader more vigorously. That population policy - linked to industrial self-sufficiency - lasted for the best part of 130 years, being replaced eventually by a mishmash of policies, ranging from the idealistic to the porkbarrel, and arousing far less public support.

Today it is frequently said that the dramatic change in immigration policy came in the 1960s and 1970s with the formal end of White Australia. On the other hand the large-scale immigration, begun in the late 1940s by Arthur Calwell (Labor) and continued by Harold Holt (Liberal), was at least as revolutionary. It moved the nation's traditional migration policy from an emphasis on the British Isles to an emphasis on people from continental Europe. Unusual in the world's history, it actually paid most of the fares and the costs of resettlement of people of alien languages and nationalities. By 1960 the two biggest groups of continental migrants were those from nations which had recently been enemies in an all-out war, Italy and Germany.

It is no longer easy to evaluate Calwell's work. In his own way he was a citizen of the world, though perhaps a less internationalist world than today's. Understandably there is a tendency to disparage Calwell, and yet his policies overall were at least as tolerant as the population and citizenship policies pursed today by the nations from which most of his ethnic critics have come.

As a Minister, Calwell boisterously upheld the White Australia Policy in public while privately allowing many Asian people to enter or stay here. He had a rasping voice, a lightning wit and a Keatingite gift for pithy phrase, and his memory is haunted by a witty aside which he made in the Federal Parliament in 1947. Justifying his decision to expel a Chinese refugee named Wong, he went on to say that: "There are many Wongs in the Chinese community, but I have to say - and I am sure that the honourable member for Balaclava will not mind me doing so - that *two Wongs do not make a White*." White was actually the name of the distinguished member for Balaclava, active in the debate.

It is a sign of the over-zealous crusade against Calwell that the quotation is never quoted without being torn from context. In retrospect it would have been better if he had been less witty. On the other hand, much of today's self-righteous commentary against him is unfair, for he was a compassionate spokesman on behalf of Aborigines and a supporter of the Indonesians in their struggles against Holland.

The 1940s is a difficult decade to discuss, in the light of later fashions in ideas and today's preferences and prejudices. In some ways Australia of the 1940s was far superior to that of today, just as in other ways it was far inferior: all depends on the standards by which a society is judged.

Therefore it is not easy to accept the widely held view of younger members of the media that Australian life must have been *intellectually* boring until the arrival of street cafes, television, the cooks of all nations, flourishing opera and ballet, the pill, careers for women, a vigorous green movement, and universities open to nearly all.

Serious public debate flourished more in the late 1940s than today. The topics of communism versus individualism, the churches versus secularism and the so-called "brave new world" versus the tired old world, were discussed more intensely, and absorbed the minds and emotions of a higher proportion of the people, than any comparable list of topics today. Most topics of debate were flavoured by the fact that the 1940s was the last decade in which both the Protestant and the Catholic churches dominated or permeated many facets of daily and political life. In the following decade Catholicism still flourished - the split of the Labor Party was a sign of its influence - but Protestantism was in some trouble; and its long control of such social matters as gambling laws and hotel laws was about to be loosened.

The end of the war spurred a belief that Australia could be reshaped. The phrase "the new order" was almost the catchcry of the mid-1940s. How to make the nation a fit place for returning heroes was the theme of countless books and pamphlets. This burst of utopianism and plain enthusiasm was reflected in the swing to the left in politics. Presbyterian and Methodist pulpits held many Ministers who thought that maybe a semi-socialist paradise on earth was now attainable. Catholic bishops in contrast preached that communism was Satan. The business monopoly, privately or publicly owned, was another of their enemies.

To many Australians, international peace now seemed an attainable goal. Maybe the new United Nations Organization could achieve it. When, in 1948, Dr H.V. Evatt, Minister for External Affairs, began his brief term as President of the general assembly of the United Nations in Paris, there was some pride even amongst many of his political opponents. But the shadow of the atomic bomb, first used in 1945, weighed heavily on people's minds - probably more so than today when nuclear weapons are infinitely more explosive.

Optimism in Australia came partly from the surge of prosperity and full employment. The abundance of food for almost everyone, though a few items were still rationed, surprised many families who had been poor as long as they could remember. There was even a new optimism towards personal health. Tuberculosis at last seemed conquerable, and in 1948 the leaders of a campaign to eradicate it predicted total victory within 20 years.

The 1940s now stand out as a high political and economic watershed. It was in wartime 1942 that the states ceased to collect their own income taxes and instead the present centralised system of taxing was imposed. Nothing did more to cement the power of Canberra. The 1940s also witnessed an extension of social security, after a quarter century in which little additional public aid, except to wounded soldiers and war widows, was offered to those in need. The 1940s also experienced a peak of a trend towards state ownership which, at the beginning of the century, had extended further in Australia and New Zealand than in almost any other nation.

The attempt after the war by Joseph Benedict Chifley, new Prime Minister (1945-49), to nationalise the trading banks and interstate airlines, thus enlarging the role of governments, was the peak of an ideological cycle which is now moving - with the sale of Qantas and the Commonwealth Bank and possibly Telstra - in the opposite direction.

Chifley's campaign to eliminate private banks aroused intense hostility but it was a hallmark of the times that the nation's leader could travel with virtually no security guard. In 1948, aged 17, I was hitch-hiking on the side of a road near Yass when along came a government car with Chifley sitting next to the driver but no other passenger and no sign of security. (Quite rightly he did not pick up the hitch-hiker)

Chifley must have been on his way to Bathurst, for he was not only Prime Minister but also an unpaid part-time councillor in a small rural shire near Bathurst. Miraculously, he continued to combine the two elected posts, and sometimes he would leave Canberra and his Prime Ministerial duties in the hours of darkness and travel across the ranges to attend a meeting of the Abercrombie Shire Council at little Perthville at 9.30 am.

A clear sign that nationally he was in grave danger of electoral defeat came in December 1947, when he lost his long-held seat at the shire elections.

The 1940s was also a miracle because it brought full employment after a lean era. In the half century from 1890 to 1940, Australia did not experience full employment even in one year. It is unlikely, though the official statistics are imperfect, that there was even one year when unemployment (by the present definition) fell below four per cent. In many years it was far above 10 per cent, and as there was usually no social security payment, the loss of a permanent job was a blow which eventually fell on children, many of whom then walked to school in bare feet.

The unemployment reached about 30 per cent in the world depression, of the early 1930s before falling sharply. In July 1939, just before the outbreak of the Second World War, about 12 per cent of wage earners were out of work. As the war effort gathered pace, the workless almost vanished. There was an acute shortage of labour, and hundreds of thousands of women were brought from the house to the paid workforce.

Many economists feared that when the war ended there would come, as happened after the previous war, a short burst of high unemployment. But the services-people took off their uniforms and instantly found work in shops, foundries, road gangs, offices, schools and almost every occupation. "During the past year," said Chifley in July 1946, "over 500,000 men and women have been released from defence and other government occupations. Yet at no stage has there been any significant number of unemployed." It was an astonishing feat. In percentage terms it is the equivalent of Australia finding jobs between Easter and Christmas next year for every person who is now unemployed.

For almost 30 years Australia was to be close to full employment. This is the startling but rarely mentioned contrast between Australia of the short Chifley and long Menzies reign and Australia in the last 20 years. In the first period Australia could boast that year after year it had less unemployment than in the USA. In the second period Australia was the poor performer, while often disguising its poor record with idle boasts.

Another striking change of the 1940s could only be glimpsed at that time. There was a turnaround in the climate of that south-eastern corner of the continent which produced most of the nation's wool and food. Between, say, the late 1880s and the mid-1940s that huge area of Australia tended to have an abnormal number of severe droughts. For much of that era farms were as important as factories, and so the unfavourable climate could wither the whole economy.

Even in the war years the droughts were extensive. Melbourne was occasionally covered with dust blown from the Mallee and Riverina. Then from the mid-1940s came at least three decades of more favourable weather in that vast productive triangle east of a line roughly drawn from Rockhampton to Port Augusta. It is now almost forgotten that the National (Country) Party in those drier years had a strong radical wing. In Victoria, the most industrialised state, the Country Party ruled from 1935 to 1945, and for most of those years it was backed by Labor.

One of the three or four main reasons for the new flavour in Federal politics after 1949 was the climate. The long reign of Sir Robert Menzies (1949-1966) owed much to the rainfall - along with higher rural prices - and the consequent rightwards swing in the big phalanx of regional seats. Malcolm Fraser entered Federal politics by winning a rural Labor seat which thereafter he retained. Significantly, the return of Labor under Bob Hawke in 1983 was partly aided by drought.

December 1949 was a watershed in Federal politics. The second-longest period of Labor rule (eight years compared to the 13 Hawke-Keating years) came to an end, and there began under Menzies the longest period of Coalition rule which was to extend to 23 years. With hindsight it now seems inevitable, but in many years of the 1940s the Liberals seemed to be condemned to an everlasting wilderness while Menzies himself, in the eyes of a section of the media and his own party, seemed likely to be replaced as leader by Richard G. Casey, the recent governor of Bengal.

It was also in 1949, before the landmark Federal election, that the power of Communists in key trade unions was dramatically weakened by the decision of Chifley to use soldiers to halt the dislocating strike on the northern coalfields of New South Wales. Communists' influence was probably weakened even more in the coal mining, waterside and other unions by the rising strength of the industrial group movement, of which B.A. Santamaria was the intellectual pilot.

The 10th of December, 1949 was also the birthday of a new method of voting which was ultimately to confer unexpected power on Cheryl Kernot, Brian Harradine, the Dark Greens and other Senate minorities. Hitherto elections for the Senate were conducted on a first-past-the-post system in which one party tended to win all senators in each state. This system often produced lopsided Senates, culminating in 1947-49 when the 36 senators consisted of 33 Labor and three from the Coalition. That meant that when a bout of the influenza swept through Canberra a debate in the Senate was even more a charade. With the winner taking all, the election of an independent or a member of a minor party to a Senate seat was virtually impossible.

The present formula of voting for senators by proportional representation was launched at the general election of 1949. Contrary to predictions, the Senate slowly became more independent, a house of review and of skirmishing. From the 1970s it was the reality rather than the exception that the government of the day did not fully control the Senate. The political crisis of November 1975, and the deposing of Mr Whitlam, would not have happened if the old system of electing the Senate had remained unaltered. Ironically, that constitutional crisis was one of the unintended effects of Chifley's attempt to reform the Senate in 1949.

Each decade creates its own splashes and radiating ripples. In creating the institutions of a new nation, the first decade of this century was crucial. In awakening national pride, Gallipoli and events of the second decade of this century were crucial. The 1960s - and the changes in Catholicism, the rise of infant green and feminist movements, the rallies against the Vietnam War, the pill, the revived concern for Aboriginal welfare - did perhaps more than any other decade to shape Australia's present culture. As for the 1980s, they are too recent to be assessed.

IN OUR TIME

The 1940s, from today's perspective, stands out as the most influential of decades. For a nation to face extinction is the loudest of all wake-up calls. So much that happened in the following years was a response to that crisis.

The Australian Magazine, 12-13 October, 1996

Forgetting the Way to Church

The decline in the habit of going to church is one of the striking changes in the last half century, and the speed of the decline has bewildered many Australians who have lived long enough to see it.

According to the latest surveys, only a quarter of the population go to church at least once a month, whereas at the end of the Second World War, maybe half of the people went to church with some regularity. Without doubt the churches then had a stronger influence in every facet of social life and many facets of political life; and an alert opinion pollster periodically tested Catholics and Baptists and others to see whether their voting intentions were altering.

In those days, most voters knew the religion, or professed religion, of those running for the highest offices, whether Federal or state, and deemed it a matter of relevance that Prime Minister Ben Chifley was a Catholic and his wife, so it was whispered, was a Presbyterian.

Those who did not go near a church and tuned into radio around 11am on Sunday and hoped to find alternatives to divine service or Sankey's sacred songs, had to fiddle the knob a few times to find something else.

The idea of a packed crowd of South Australians sitting at the football late on Sunday afternoon to watch Adelaide versus Collingwood would have been inconceivable in the 1950s for more than one reason. A law, usually called the Sabbath Observance Act, operated in every self-respecting state to ban spectator sport on a Sunday while many municipal councils banned any activity on their ovals and tennis courts on Sunday. In "solid" country areas, the farmer who ploughed on Sunday was asking for frowns in the nearest town, to be followed by divine wrath around harvest time.

It sounds strait-laced and joyless, and it some places it was, but the Australian society of that period probably functioned more effectively than it does today and possessed at least as strong a sense of fun and fulfilment as the wealthier and more liberated society that has not only supplanted it but, periodically looking back, tends to poke fun at it.

Why the churches have declined so rapidly is a matter of debate. Clearly in those years they did not have to compete with rival entertainments on Sunday. Nobody owned a television set and most families did not yet own a car that could take them on a Sunday outing. Shops, except milkbars, were closed, sports grounds and cinemas were closed, and hotels, of course, were locked except for the bona-fide travellers, and they were few.

Suburban churches were popular meeting places, just as they still are in farming areas. The social life of a couple of million families revolved around churches and their clubs and other activities.

Religion has probably suffered even more from the remarkable social changes since the 1960s, including attitudes to sex, marriage, divorce, abortion, teenagers, women, the family, parental discipline, birth, death, alcohol, drugs, nature, work and leisure. All these were activities on which most churches held forceful views, and now those views are challenged or ignored.

Possibly the quickest and most sweeping social revolution in the history of the human race, it also widened a generation gap. A whole generation is missing in many of the old major churches. The survivors of the age group born before 1918 are well-represented in church, but the millions belonging to the age group born since 1958 are not. If it were the other way round, the churches would be crammed.

Some observers see the Christian churches — but not Islam — as in their twilight in the Western world. I doubt if this interpretation is backed by strong evidence. The religion so central to Western civilisation still has power in its batteries. At the other extreme, some Christian observers reassure themselves by explaining away the declining numbers in Australia as largely the result of the welcome departure of people who sat in church for the "wrong reason" - Catholics who were scared of hell and Protestants who chased the "social niceties".

Neither the pessimists nor the optimists are convincing. A wide range of factors affects the churches. Their long-term vigor in Australia remains an open question.

Age, 4 September, 1993

IN OUR TIME

Does the Future Belong to a Galaxy of Smaller Nations?

The topics under the name of nationalism are so entangled that it is hazardous to pluck out conclusions of contemporary relevance. But some issues seem to lend themselves to predictions.

One crucial topic is whether a sense of nationality will increasingly shape the world's maps during the next 50 years. In the opinion of some observers — and events in Yugoslavia and the Russian borders give them fuel — the big-area nations are giving way to smaller nations based on a sense of common ties of language, race, and history.

Force and threat helped to create the big empires and nations, especially in the 19th and earlier centuries. This was more or less true of czarist Russia and the Soviet Union, of the United States, India, China, and a variety of other nations occupying large territories. Likewise, the colonial empires could not have been built up by European sea powers without their fighting strength. In the last 45 or more years, however, these maritime empires have been shattered into pieces.

Nationalism was one motivator of the fragmentation but far from the only factor. The economic and military decline of Britain, France, Holland, Portugal, and other colonial powers aided the process. The new superpowers, the United States and the Soviet Union, smiled on the process, not realizing that ultimately they too could be affected by it.

The process of nationalist fragmentation might well become strong within the big-area countries. What is happening in the former Soviet territories could well occur in China, where there are sharp ethnic and regional differences. China also experiences a stark contrast in the pace of economic development in the city ports on the one hand and the western interior on the other. Breakaways in the west of the United States and the north of Australia are conceivable in the next 50 years. India and Pakistan have already experienced cleavages.

Generally, a time of international tension, with a high fear of wars between the major powers, puts a brake on secession and national independence movements, especially within the sphere of influence of the big powers. It is unlikely that today's relatively peaceful and more relaxed relations between major powers will last long. New tensions could well be accompanied by a renewal of consolidation in place of the present nationalist fragmentation.

Since 1945 a multitude of independent nations has arisen, most of them appealing to or kindling a sense of nationalism; but it would be a mistake to see them as essentially an expression of a heightened sense of nationality in the world. Significantly, the last 25 years have seen a growing sense of what might be labeled "global nationalism", a sense that the world is one. It throbs in the conservation movement—in the Dark Greens more than in the Light Greens. In advanced economies an influential minority believes that the tropical rainforests belong to the whole world. With the growth of international tourism has come a wide veneration for places of natural beauty, irrespective of the nation that owns them. Traditionally, nationalism has thrived on a narrower sense of belonging, a belief that a particular mountain, valley, or coastal bluff is a nation's own shrine.

There was an earlier wave of "global nationalism"—a veneration for nature everywhere and for those "primitive" peoples living close to nature irrespective of their national location — in the Romantic era. It reappeared between about the years 1890 to 1910. The marchers in that later movement included the new Boy Scouts, the Russian ballet, jazz, cubism, Frazer's *Golden Bough,* Tarzan, Gauguin, *The Call of the Wild,* and *The Rite of Spring.* That international movement ran out of steam before the First World War, a warning that the present powerful Nature Revival might not always run strongly. Many Dark Green disciples see "global nationalism" as a running mate of oldtime nationalism and often fitter.

It is far from certain that the future belongs to a multitude of nations. The history of the Australian Aborigines offers one comment about far past and distant future. After the first Europeans settled at Sydney in 1788, they had the chance to observe an entire continent still following the semi-nomadic but systematic economy of hunting and gathering. Prehistoric Australia was a clue to the world's way of life before the beginnings of the neolithic revolution some 10,000 years ago: before the twin innovations of the domesticating of plants and of animals transformed the world with even more effect than the industrial revolution.

The continent of Australia, in 1788 and probably 10,000 years earlier, held about 600 tribes and territories, most of which could loosely be labeled "national" as much as tribal. (Probably the prehistoric California also had 300.) These roughly fitted Sir Alan Bullock's definition of nationalism—"the feeling of belonging to a group united by common racial, linguistic, and historical ties, and usually identified with a particular territory". It is likely that in the seminomadic era of human history, the inhabited world held at least 25,000 territories with many of the characteristics of present nations and a powerful sense of belonging. Today, in contrast, the world has fewer than 200 nations, though the number grows.

Is the recent increase in independent nations a temporary fact, the product of a period of relative international peace? Will the world in the year 2092 be divided into relatively few nations? For the first time in the history of mankind it is almost possible, in the prevailing technology of communications and armaments, for one nation or government to dominate the globe, though not necessarily to maintain a long-term dominance. Ten thousand years ago, in contrast, there was no strong division of labor, scant hoarding of food, virtually no defensive works worthy of the name, no facility for an army of even 100 fighters to travel far, and no opportunity for conquering a tribe or "nation" living, say, 400 miles away. Of course there were wars, but no capacity for creating a big-area tribe or nation except in unwanted desert.

In our era of well-nourished nationalism, when the nation and the independence it confers are valued highly by most human beings, there is also a possibility of world government. It might well be imposed by force or pressured agreement in the next 100 years. Technology is now making possible what even in 1900 was impossible.

This does not necessarily mean that world government will emerge or that a couple of superpowers will gain sway over nearly all the world. But what is possible may well be occasionally attempted. Perhaps we should not be too confident in thinking that the future belongs to a galaxy of nations and all the satisfactions and independence—and scope for international conflict—they offer.

"The Worth of Nations", a conversazione at Boston University, 12-14 November, 1992

This Marvellous, Calamitous Century

The world 100 years ago was, materially and mentally, almost as close to the era of Christ as it is to the era of Clinton. That simple assessment sums up how sweeping and momentous have been the changes in the 20th century.

Many of those changes, whether sobering or pleasing, were not predicted. In 1900 Europe ruled most of the world - few observers could have predicted that a century later a host of independent nations would exist in Africa and Asia, let alone the Pacific Islands. In 1900 democracy was in its infancy and still a rarity. It is now difficult to conceive that then only a handfull of nations gave all men the right to vote. and not one nation gave women both the right to vote and to stand for Parliament.

Full-blooded democracy still remains a brave new experiment, the history of ancient Athens notwithstanding. It would be unwise to assume that its victory across the globe is inevitable, for democracy is not always a simple mode of governing. It is almost forgotten that one reason why in this century the world stood three times on the verge of chaos - during two world wars and one world depression - was that the leading democracies were almost as prone to accidents and blunders as were their authoritarian rivals.

During the first half of this century, two shattering wars dominated the debit side of the globe's balance sheet. Miraculously, there has been no war involving two major powers since the Korean War of the 1950s. The end of the mis-named Cold War in 1990 has given the tail years of this century almost an air of serenity, and there are some grounds for predicting that the next century will be less shadowed by war. That there will be wars, middle-ranking as well as minor, in the 21st century is almost beyond doubt.

Amongst the cluster of far-reaching changes in this century, some observers would give priority to the changed role of women and marriage. In 1900 the word "spinster" was seen as synonymous with failure. A woman in the professions was a rarity, except in teaching. A woman in a Parliament was unknown, though the Queen of the largest empire in the world was concluding a "term of office" longer than any female Prime Minister is ever likely to experience.

Other observers of this vanishing century would emphasise the decline of organised religion within the prosperous nations. Dominant for thousands of years, religion did not seem likely to decline so quickly. It is doubtful, however, whether the decline is permanent.

The last 100 years have seen an astonishing change in medicine and health. At least half of the world's people experience a length of life unparalleled by their ancestors. This is presumably one of the causes of the decline of most churches in the west. Religion flourished more—it was a walking stick and a source of inspiration—when daily life was short, perilous, and more often painful.

The ever-expanding city is now displacing the countryside as the home of most of the world's people. Throughout human history, nearly all the people had lived in the countryside. They were profoundly influenced by the alternation of winter and summer, by the coming and going of the full moon and crescent moon, and by the pattern of rain and the annual harvest: if their harvest failed, they starved or half-starved. Now Africa remains the only continent so vulnerable to the stresses and pressures once prevailing everywhere.

The 20th century experienced an extraordinary change in the daily activities of at least half of the world's people. Hard, unremitting physical labour had dominated their life. Even a century ago the hard work necessary to produce food and shelter and clothing was a lifelong task, both for women and men; and the penalties for failure were devastating,

The machine and other new techniques of production have transformed work. In one sense the widespread unemployment of today is an indictment of political organization, but is it is also a sign of the triumph of the economic system, faulty as it is. In Europe alone scores of millions of people are no longer needed to produce the necessities of life. The typical unemployed people in the typical western land have a higher standard of living than that of their great grandparents who laboured 60 hours a week in Athens or Berlin at the start of this century. To point this out is not to condone unemployment but to emphasise how its character has altered.

It is a mirror of the extraordinary spread of leisure, wanted and unwanted, that spectator sport is almost becoming the international language. Whereas in 1900 there were few international sporting contests that aroused public interest - the Olympic Games was still a minor carnival - today the grand international sporting fixtures show signs of serving as the focus for a lot of the national pride and aggression that went into war.

Another surprise of the last 100 years is the enthroning of nature. It is almost the new religion. Though there were foretastes of this mode of worship in the 1890s, nature's winning of converts in the prosperous nations during the last third of a century has been on an unexpectedly large scale.

The enthroning of nature is partly an effect of a shrinking world, of a new inter-dependence. And yet the shrinking world seems to pull nations and people in two directions. It promotes internationalism. It also promotes a strong sense of locality and nationalism. That tug-o-war will form one of the tensions of the coming century.

The Age, 26 October, 1998

IN OUR TIME

Mr Gibbon's Decline and Fall

The *Decline and Fall of the Roman Empire* is in some ways the most astonishing history book ever written.

Its author, Edward Gibbon, put down his pen at the finish of the final volume a few months before the First Fleet reached Botany Bay. And here is his work, 200 years later, again appearing in print, unaltered, in an edition designed not just for the specialists but for a small regiment of intelligent readers who have a hankering to read this famous book and—with determination—probably will succeed.

Nearly every person with an old-fashioned education nods approvingly when Gibbon is talked about. Some actually have read him. I confess I had skimmed only sections—maybe 300 pages in all—until the arrival of this edition made me sit down and read, here and there skipping a page. The six volumes, packed into two neat boxes, run to about 4000 pages in this Everyman's Edition.

The Everyman reprints, mostly classics, were once to be found in nearly every house possessing a bookshelf. In an era when many people carried a book in their pocket to read in the train or while taking a walk, these books were ever so handy. This edition is really the version that Everyman's first issued in 1910 but in a larger format, with a clearer and more attractive typeface and the advantage of two fine introductions, placed at the start of volumes one and four, by the English historian Hugh Trevor-Roper. The maps in this edition, are alas, dreary and mean.

When Edward Gibbon first planned these books he was embarking on an intellectual voyage that was central to his century. To this Englishman born at Putney on the Thames in 1737, the world of the Romans seemed a triumph. Of the world's great empires, the British Empire could not yet be compared to the Roman.

Gibbon praised the Roman empire with a loudspeaker-like emphasis: "If a man were called to fix the period in the history of the world during which the condition of the human race was most happy and prosperous, he would, without hesitation, name that which elapsed from the death of Domitian to the accession of Commodus. The vast extent of the Roman Empire was governed by absolute power, under the guidance of virtue and wisdom. The armies were restrained by the firm but gentle hand of four successive emperors, whose characters and authority commanded involuntary respect." He added that the "image of liberty" and the belief in civic virtue were other hallmarks of the Roman heyday that ended about AD 179.

Today it would be hard to find an historian who would adjudicate with pontifical certainty about one of the most difficult questions in human history - when did the human race enjoy its golden age?

The Roman empire and its remarkable civilization were followed by what Gibbon called the "most awful scene in the history of mankind". It was therefore appropriate for him to wonder why the Roman empire had collapsed so dismally and whether the equally proud civilization of the Europe of his day might eventually be followed by another Dark Age. He was fairly confident that Europe of the Enlightenment would continue to flourish. His view of the future would have been less cheerful if he were still writing when the French Revolution erupted.

There was not much in Gibbon's background and early childhood to suggest that his native talent would one day be combined with intellectual stamina and a gift for words. He was sickly as a child - the churchyard held his siblings. He was not an achiever at Oxford, from which he was sternly withdrawn when he flirted with Catholicism. Almost by a miracle he was sent by his father to the mentally-charged Swiss town that became the training ground for his abilities. Lausanne possessed earnest Calvinist pastors who believed in religious liberty. The town spoke French, a language in which Gibbon won fluency, thus gaining access to a new stream of ideas in the social sciences.

Mr Gibbon's Decline and Fall

He began to read the Frenchman, Montesquieu, who believed that history was the product of a variety of secular causes including climate and political and social customs. Montesquieu was to the study of history what Marx was a century later: a constructive incendiarist. Gibbon also read the Neapolitan historian and lawyer, Giannone, who sceptically traced the way the Catholic church influenced history. On the shores of the Swiss lake, under the influence of a Calvinist pastor, the 16-year-old Gibbon began to discover during the next five years—in Trevor-Roper's words—"what he had lacked in England: a philosophy to organise his vast, undigested historical reading".

Later, on his grand tour, Gibbon visited Italy. There on 15 October 1764 he had a vision. It was at Rome, he recalled, "as I sat musing amidst the ruins of the Capitol, while the barefoot friars were singing vespers in the Temple of Jupiter, that the idea of writing the decline and fall of the city first started to my mind." For years his fascination with Catholicism, and his periodic revulsions against it, was the daily medicine of his mind.

When finally in England he set himself the task of systematically reading and writing, he began with the city of Rome but increasingly embraced its vast empire. He wrote three volumes on the history of the Roman empire from its glory years until the sack of Rome, and then concluded that after all his hard labour he was entitled to say "enough". What was then intended to be his final chapter summed up his story: "The loss or desolation of the provinces from the Ocean to the Alps impaired the glory and greatness of Rome: her internal prosperity was irretrievably destroyed by the separation of Africa." And then the Vandals came.

Edward Gibbon decided to resume his history. Taking up his pen again, he carried the story of the crumbling Roman empire forward to the 15th century. He described Christianity's spread even to India, the Saxon conquest of Britain, the Goths besieging Rome, events in Persia and Ethiopia, the rise of Islam and its assaults on Constantinople, the coming of the Mongols and "Zinghis Khan" and much more.

Most of those who began to read Gibbon—and did not suffer a heart attack when they saw his unorthodox religious views—must have marvelled at his gifts. He showed the talents of a giant: prodigious reading, a willingness to argue, a capacity to bring the past to life, and a sense of the complex factors that caused great events.

Though occasionally he leaves behind a censorious or fuddy-duddy taste—the result of his unusual personality as well as the passing of two centuries—there is so much to admire in his work. We can marvel at his television-like ability to set a scene. How much more would people have marvelled at his chapters in the era when there was little foreign travel, no photography, and scant access to the paintings which depicted life in ancient Rome, thus making the printed word so important? His descriptions of scenes and places are less intimate than panoramic. It was as if he sat on a mountain and looked down.

Thus, after noting that the Romans penetrated only a short way into Scotland, he painted the unconquered Scottish highlands with a few scratches of his quill pen. These Roman masters of the known world, he wrote, "turned with contempt from gloomy hills assailed by the winter tempest, from lakes concealed in a blue mist, and from cold and lonely heaths, over which the deer of the forest were chased by a troop of naked barbarians".

Here is the embryo script-writer of the big-screen. We are shown Attila the Hun with "large head, a swarthy complexion, small deep-seated eyes, a flat nose, a few hairs in the place of a beard, broad shoulders, and a short square body, of nervous strength, though of a short disproportioned form". We learn too that Attila had the habit of "fiercely rolling his eyes, as if he wished to enjoy the terror he inspired".

We follow the love life of Antonia, wife of the general Belisarius; and we see the general himself leading Roman soldiers so disciplined that they do not pilfer or pillage. When he marched them through the countryside in the 6th century, not an apple was stolen from orchards and no destructive pathway was cut through a ripening field of grain by these thousands of tramping feet.

We see the former Syrian shepherd Simeon Stylites sitting atop his column 60 feet high, through 30 summers and winters. With no fear of giddiness this holy man prays almost mechancially day after day, "bending his meagre skeleton from the forehead to the feet", and performing that ritual at least 1240 times in succession, according to one spectator. Gibbon usually stands some physical distance from the events he describes. His camera is not often close-up.

When he describes cruelty in all its variations, whether flaying alive or the act of killing, he rarely goes into squeamish details. Thus the insolvent debtors are described as lying in prison with 12 ounces of rice a day and bound with a 15-pound chain. After 60 days in prison they are "either put to death or sold in foreign slavery beyond the Tiber". At the very worst a debtor's body might be "legally dismembered"—a warning to those who thoughtlessly went into debt. Now we know why there were few high-flying entrepreneurs in ancient Rome.

During the course of Gibbon's book, Christianity spreads. He has no time for the monasteries, and the platoons of monks are parasites in his eyes. The doctrine of the Trinity he calls a late impostor, appearing long after the time of Christ. He thinks most of the miracles that impressed the masses were tricks.

While in some ways Gibbon was hostile to early Christianity he saw a role for a simple religion. It laid down duties and responsibilities which, to Gibbon far more than to Canberra today, were the backbone of civilization. Christianity, he admitted, had a "pure and genuine influence" on the barbarians of northern Europe. While the conversion of Constantine to Christianity served to weaken the Roman empire, it also "mollified the ferocious temper" of the savage conquerors who swarmed down from the north.

There is modernity in many of his views. He showed sympathys for the Jews. Not a narrow patriot, he saw Europe in the 1780s as "one great republic, whose various inhabitants have attained almost the same level of politeness and cultivation". He believed that all or nearly all races had potential and he admired the Romans who—unlike the Greeks—refused to follow the "narrow policy of preserving, without any foreign mixture, the pure blood of the ancient citizens". Gibbon applauded the Romans for conferring their ultimate privileges on strangers and barbarians. His applause did not go to the Libyans who were "the most savage of mankind".

In his thoughts on history he favours a cyclical view. What goes up will probably come down. Success leads to pride which creates complacency. Austerity can pave the way to prosperity and luxury which germinate the seeds of decay.

Of the Romans, he concluded that their final decline "was the natural and inevitable effect of immoderate greatness. Prosperity ripened the principle of decay". Likewise, the Turks of the 6th century, he claims, "were enervated by luxury, which is always fatal except to an industrious people". Such views were more widely held by Gibbon than by today's historians. To my mind, however, those views have some merit.

Gibbon's literary skill is a crucial ingredient of his success. At his best he sets the dry silent past on fire again. Quaint events and snatches of curious detail he passes on to his reader with enthusiasm. He can be slightly dull for a page or two but it is partly the stolid sequence of events he is sometimes obliged to describe that lays down a temporary blanket of dullness.

His prose is not discussed in detail in Trevor-Roper's editorial comments. To my mind Gibbon's prose is like a slow procession moving in stately manner along a highway, not so slow as to be dull and not so fast as to be overheated. The rhythm of his prose is powerful, and the way the complications of the story are dovetailed into a continuous narrative show a master carpenter at work. But those who prefer to read short paragraphs will be dismayed to see that some of his paragraphs, as was the fashion, run for five pages.

It is remarkable that after 200 years Gibbon can still be read with relative ease. In the books hardly one word in 5000—and these are likely to be theological, military or specialist words—calls for a dictionary. A hallmark of his prose is the constant use of paired or balancing nouns, adjectives and phrases. He does not feel at home with the lone adjective or noun. And so people are "rude and corrupt"; their minds are "inquisitive and ambitious", they retreat to the "church and cloister" or to "the pursuits and pleasures of a secular life". All these paired words are taken from the same half page in volume six. To me these pairs, these twins, add more to the music, the drumbeat, of his sentences than to the meaning intended. They are part of the theatre in which Gibbon is the great actor-producer.

Gibbon is still admired for the same reason that the novels of Anthony Trollope are read. Here is an author who is gracious, cultivated, usually humane, elegant with words, skilled in telling a story, and willing to take endless pains in order to make the reader feel at home. Though many pages are filled with war and civil violence and some with cruelty and chaos, he himself breathes moderation and calm and composure, so that the civilised manner of the author on the one hand and the uncivilised events he often describes on the other hand, seem to belong to different worlds. It is that pairing which is part of the fascination.

Whom should Gibbon be compared with? I sometimes liken him to Arnold Toynbee in the sweep of his story, but he is more instinctively an historian than Toynbee. Gibbon is probably unique. His is not a book to solve arguments that depend on accuracy, for knowledge changes and grows over 200 years. But he is generally accurate and he is wary of being taken in by his source material. To emphasise his visible literary gifts is to run the risk of minimising his invisible talents as an historian.

Gibbon knew he had accomplished a task of importance though he was too urbane to proclaim that positively. His own account of how in 1787 he ended after 20 years his sustained labour of composition is one of the most moving passages in literary history. In his *Memoirs* he recalled how towards midnight on a balmy evening, in a summer house in his garden in Switzerland, he wrote the last lines. After putting down his pen, he began to stroll along the covered walk of acacia trees, with the lake and the mountains standing out before him: "The air was temperate, the sky was serene, the silver orb of the moon was reflected from the waters, and all Nature was silent. I will not dissemble the first emotions of joy on recovery of my freedom, and, perhaps the establishment of my fame. But my pride was soon humbled, and a sober melancholy was spread over my mind, by the idea that I had taken an everlasting leave of an old and agreeable companion."

Taking the manuscript of volumes four to six, he travelled across France to the English Channel and so to England where he spent much of the autumn correcting the proofs. The last volumes came out in 1788, on his 51st birthday. He died five years later.

One English summer, hiring a car at Brighton, we went into the countryside and came across the village where Gibbon is buried. The old church was unlocked, and his ornate burial place was visible in the dark and eccentric interior. He is not a cult figure, tourists do not pour into the church, and so, as he might have wished, he is alone. To write such great history, especially to write it while belonging to no institution and rarely attending even a public library, is a rare and a lonely feat. It is right that he should be alone.

Independent Monthly, August 1995

Part 2
Partly Personal

The First Christmas I Remember

The first Christmas clear in my memory must have been 1934 when I was four. We lived in Gippsland, and one of our grandfathers was coming.

We went to the station to meet him. To our astonishment he went to the end of the steam train and produced from the guard's van a bicycle. We children could not understand why he had put his bike in the train rather than ridden it. We presumably did not know that Melbourne was so far away from Leongatha.

There was a sensation when our dad, in preparation for Christmas dinner, went out to the woodheap and put the head of a white leghorn on the chopping block and axed it with a sharp blow. The chook fluttered about without its head. All over Victoria on Christmas Eve, gory scenes were witnessed in back yards.

Our mum plucked the chook, using boiling water. I got a feather and wore it in my hair. Poultry was a luxury in those days and eaten only in one meal in the year by most families.

The high point of Christmas dinner — it was lunchtime — was the hot pudding. We were told to watch out for a hidden threepenny bit. The coin was so small and was easily camouflaged by the brownish, sticky pudding. The joy of finding one!

I have long forgotten what Christmas present I received. This was the era of the cheap brightly colored tin toy. They were small and flimsy, and were ricketty by Boxing Day. But the couple of days when their tiny wheels stayed on or their clockwork engine actually worked were wonderful.

IN OUR TIME

Christmas was the one day of the year we really celebrated.

Sunday Age, 22 December, 1991

Ballarat

In 1941 we moved from Geelong to Ballarat. I had just turned 11. Here I first saw snow—an astonishing sight. I am not sure whether I had previously known that it occasionally snowed in Australia—hence my surprise at the white on the grass and the intense cold.

As labour was scarce during the war it was easy to find part-time work, and every Saturday I worked for a fruiterer who drove a green panel van filled with fruit, cabbages and potatoes.

He went in to a customer's house and took the orders, a pencil behind his ear. I delivered the purchases in a basket—nothing was wrapped—to the back door while he drove his van on to the next customer. I collected the cash in a leather bag and followed on the bike.

One of his older customers was probably the first author I ever met. He was Nathan Spielvogel and was well known for his book, *Gumsucker on the Tramp*.

I learned to know every street in Ballarat, except a few in Sebastopol. I also kept chooks and knew the price of bran, pollard, wheat and eggs.

I used my vast earnings to buy a tiny secondhand metal canoe and paddle on the lake. Not on Sunday of course because that day in Ballarat was silent, being dominated by the dozens of churches and all their activities.

Here I became interested in history. The sight of all those old buildings and the gorse-covered mullock heaps and the big cemeteries made me conscious of another era. I learned little about Ballarat's history while I lived there (the relevant books were few, and out of print) but I remained curious, knowing there must be a history.

I feel I owe a lot to Ballarat.

The opening of an address at Ballarat, 1996

IN OUR TIME

Snippet: Who is the Typical Australian?

It's difficult in the 1980s and '90s to pick a quintessential modern Australian. I think you'd be justified in 1810 in saying the convict was the quintessential Australian. In the 1850s I think most people would say the gold-digger was the quintessential Australian; there were so many of them and they were successful. Maybe in 1900 the small farmer was the quintessential Australian. They were a minority but they and their families formed nearly a quarter of the population and they were distinctive in many ways. You might have said that in World War II the soldier and the war worker were the quintessential Australian because the tasks they were doing were so important and they were representative.

But I think at the moment you couldn't pick the quintessential Australian. For one thing, women would be part of it when previously they weren't. That makes it even more difficult to find a category or a job or a work group. The proportion of people living in the Outback is so small, the farming population is so small, manufacturing is no longer quintessential. Maybe the quintessential Australian is a public servant on a sickie, but that's not fair because most of them are not on sickies.

Adelaide Advertiser, 26 January, 1991

IN OUR TIME

A Few Words at a Funeral

Hilda May Lanyon was born in East Gippsland, in the remote settlement of Buchan South, on 10 November, 1903. The house in which she was born was made of stringybark, having been built by a pioneer who had vanished to the W.A. goldfields. When it rained heavily, the roof leaked. The surrounding hills were so steep that supplies were brought to the house in a horse-drawn sledge.

Her father, Henry Maynard Lanyon, was the only teacher at the nearby school. When he was told by the local midwife that the birth of our mother could be difficult he rode his bike five miles to the nearest post office and sent a reply-paid telegram to the doctor, 20 miles away. The doctor came from Bruthen on horseback, but by then the baby was born. "I came into a loving home," Mum once wrote.

The family moved to Corryong where she first went to school. Corryong was almost as isolated as Buchan, and one day there was a sensation in the schoolroom when the loud noise of a motor car was heard from the street and the children climbed onto the desks to look at this strange vehicle that would change the world. She once recalled that on her sixth birthday, in 1909, old Grandma Wilkinson - an immigrant of the goldrush years - was staying in the house. At the birthday party she taught the children how to play the exciting game, "Here we come looby-lo". As Mum recorded in a note: "On Saturday night after tea my grandmother carefully gathered our toys, put them in a box, and covered them with a cloth so 'Satan won't tempt you to play with them on Sunday'." But after breakfast on Sunday, when old grandma wasn't looking, the mother rescued a few toys for the children.

Before the First World War the Lanyon family moved to Gisborne, then a village. There the father was to become absorbed in Esperanto, the language expected to solve the world's problems. Our mother and the older children learned to speak and write it. Before long Mum, still a child, was conducting a correspondence with scores of Esperantists in the Austro-Hungarian empire and many other lands. Much of the family income must have been spent on postcards and penny stamps.

From Gisborne state school she won a scholarship to Melbourne High, then a school for both boys and girls. It stood on the island in Spring Street where now the Royal College of Surgeons stands. She was very fond of the school and in later years met her old classmates at annual reunions. As a high-school girl she boarded at St Kilda, on the seafront, where one of her aunts, Aunty Em, ran a boarding house. The sayings and activities of the other boarders remained a topic of lasting conversation.

Trained as a teacher of the very young, a prizewinning student, she taught for several years in tiny schools on the northern plains. In those schools she was the only teacher. Students remembered her with affection.

After she met our father, a young Methodist Minister, she had the customary long courtship, rarely meeting him because his churches and her school were far apart. Her first of many married homes was in the Wimmera, at Jeparit. The eldest son, John, was born there; Joan and I were born while the family was in Terang; Ellis was born in Leongatha; nobody was born in Geelong; and Donald was born while we lived at Burnbank Street in Ballarat.

We were always moving, usually not knowing where our home would be until about a month before the move took place. In those days the parsonages, next door to the church, were furnished, pre-furnished to use today's jargon. Our mother longed to have, someday, a house where she could choose the furniture and the curtains and floor coverings and colour scheme. She also longed to have her own garden, grown from cuttings, which she eventually achieved in retirement.

As children we could only guess how hard she worked. I am pretty sure she did not have an ice chest until the family moved to the church of Prince of Wales Park, Thornbury, just before the end of the Second World War. She was at Dandenong sometime after 1950 when her first washing machine arrived. So for years she had been busy cooking, sweeping, bed-making, tending the wood stove, doing the washing, knitting and darning and button-sewing and ironing. Sometimes when we ran home from school we would find the kitchen table full of empty bottles ready to be filled with the new-made jam that stood in the big boiler on the wood stove. In another room she had a huge bag for the darning and mending, so large it was almost beyond her ever to reach the socks at the very bottom.

Last week one of the young nurses at the Florence Nightingale Hospital asked us what our mother had done during her life. How can you answer such a question? She did almost everything, and often on a small budget. Of course many people were kind. She once recalled with gratitude that when one of the children had an expensive operation the two doctors, Dr Judkins and Kingsley Norris, charged nothing.

She lived in the country towns in the era when notices of church meetings and socials always ended with the words, "ladies, please bring a plate". How many thousands of plates of buttered scones, Anzac biscuits, drop scones and tomato and beetroot sandwiches she must have made, just before setting out for the meetings, often with a child in one arm and a plate in the other!

In every town she was prominent in the Womens Auxiliary for Overseas Missions, the Ladies Guild, the Women's Christian Temperance Union, and other groups: usually she presided, opening the meeting with prayer. Sometimes she went with our Dad to call on farmers who belonged to the tiny rural churches in which he preached on Sunday afternoons. Visiting it was called, and a vital church duty in those days. In later years she took religious instruction in schools.

Once, when living at Mt Waverley, she was invited to be the guest on Tommy Hanlon Junior's afternoon TV show, *This is Your Life*, and many of her activities were recalled, to the delight of her friends. That day she actually brought home a plate.

Like us all she had her eccentricities but in the best sense of the word she was a good citizen of the many towns and suburbs she lived in. She took no part, however, in party politics - it would have seemed divisive in a clergyman's wife. Many of her privately-uttered political views she inherited from her mother who was a dedicated supporter of the United Australia Party in the days of J.A. Lyons and the young R.G. Menzies.

As she grew older she developed a deep respect for earlier generations of Australians, especially her own female ancestors. She absorbed herself in finding out their history. Discovering long-lost relatives on the plains of north Queensland was one of the windfalls of her later years.

Girrawheen, where she lived her last four years, she loved. There she was frequently meeting somebody who knew somebody who had once attended churches or schools in the towns and rural crossroads she or her husband once knew: in Box Hill, Noorat, Wandella, Koonwarra, Boort, Sulky Gully, Wendouree, Tarranyurk, Lovely Banks, Herne Hill, Keysborough (then rural), the church in Kooyong Road in Armadale, and here in the New Street church.

She had intense curiosity about people. To the end she also retained, somewhat to her surprise, her remarkable memory, for long ago she had thought that she was doomed to inherit what she called "the curse of the Westcotts - a failing memory".

All her Australian ancestors were Wesleyans or became so. She was proud to be a Methodist. After the Uniting Church was born she became part of it but she made it clear that she was still a Methodist. It would have given her contentment to know that a memorial service for her would be held in this church, one of the oldest Methodist churches in Australia.

New Street church, Brighton, 10 May, 1991

Grand Final: the Eagles Win

I have seen Geelong play a few hundred times, often standing all afternoon in driving rain, and so I've learned not to be too optimistic. But I held the idea on Saturday at lunchtime that they had a 50-50 chance of beating the West Coast in the Grand Final.

For almost two quarters of the match I thought Geelong might win. The West Coast's runaway after half time was all the more to their credit.

It must be one of the few times I have ever left a match a couple of minutes before the sound of what I still find myself calling "the final bell". And walking across the parklands I could hear the boos as the West Coast players paraded in triumph. It was like a gale of protest, lifted by the wind out of the high walls of the stadium.

For many months the muffled resentment and the disappointment will be heard in Victoria. I gauge that from our daughter. She came to the football when she was six or seven and liked to collect discarded paper-streamers around the goals, but she rarely watched the football thereafter.

Yesterday, imagine my surprise when she mentioned on the phone that she felt resentment at the premiership cup leaving Victoria.

Mrs Joan Kirner, the Premier, who genuinely likes the football rather than pretends to like it, carefully chose the Saturday after the Grand Final for the Victorian State election.

After Pyramid's fall and the Ford Company's retrenchments, Geelong is one of the Labor Party's sore spots. A Geelong premiership could have eased the soreness and increased Labor's vote around Corio Bay.

Indeed, a Geelong win might have added a pinch of happiness to every electorate, thus lowering the resentment widely felt against the Labor Party on the eve of the most difficult election it has faced for a long time.

The victory by the West Coast Eagles will temporarily drag the self-esteem of many Victorians a notch lower. Significantly, not one city in the United States can equal the remarkable sporting traditions of Melbourne, and not one city in Europe has a senior football team as old as Geelong's.

Alas, all Victoria has now lost the prized trophy in the very game its people invented. The Eagles' victory—and they fully deserved, it—has snatched away something vital from Victoria. Most of the 95,000 people sitting at the MCG on Saturday knew that this was the end of an era.

For me it was the end of an era but also the climax of an era. As a historian I see Western Australia as a special child, a sporting child, of Victoria. Here were the emphatic signs that the child had grown up.

By the strangest coincidence, at the very time when the West Coast captured the lead last Saturday afternoon, a special luncheon with speeches (and trannies cupped to many ears!) was being held in the famous old W.A. gold town of Coolgardie, nearly 2000 miles away. I know about it only because — but for the Grand Final—I would have been there.

On Saturday afternoon, Coolgardie was celebrating the centenary of the discovery of the gold that did more than anything to make Western Australia a new stronghold of Australian Rules, and eventually a State powerful enough to produce champions in many of the sports we play.

I am willing to bet that if we could piece together the complete family tree of the 20 West Coast Eagles who played on Saturday, we would find at least one Victorian ancestor, male or female, in over half of the team. Those ancestors had been lured west after the finding of gold at Coolgardie in 1892.

The beginnings of the fine skills that the Eagles showed on the Melbourne Cricket Ground on Saturday came mostly from Victorian footballers who had carried their footballs, boots and lace-up guernseys to Kalgoorlie and Perth in those years of gold.

Thus, Albert Thurgood would have been proud if he could have seen Saturday's Grand Final. The Gary Ablett of the last years of the last century, Thurgood caused dismay in the dressing room of the Essendon club when he said after the 1894 season that he was leaving depressed Victoria to try his luck in the west.

Essendon, the finest team of that era, missed him acutely. From his favourite position at centre-half-forward he had regularly kicked an annual 50 or more goals at a time when that probably equalled 175 goals today!

Thurgood was one of the Victorian giants who quickly lifted the game in W.A. above its first phase of paddock football. After four seasons he returned to Essendon at their old East Melbourne ground, his skills as astonishing as ever.

In the year of his return, he performed what was possibly the most astonishing feat in the history of our game. He place-kicked a football, with a little help from the wind, a distance of almost 108 yards or 98-and-a-half metres.

Year by year the quality of Perth and Kalgoorlie football improved, and some of their star footballers began to come east. When I first saw Geelong in 1937, at the old Corio Oval overlooking the salt marshes, Geelong was already plucking stars from the west.

A long procession of them played for Geelong, a glory to the team. They included George Moloney who kicked over 100 goals in a season, Polly Farmer and his miraculous palming of the ball, Marshall and Watts, Peake, Malarkey, and Saturday's captain, Mark Bairstow, a noble son of the wheatbelt of W.A.

Barracking for Geelong, you can't think too harshly of W.A. It has been a fertile recruiting ground not just for competent players but for those stylish individualists who have come to be regarded almost as substitutes for premierships at Kardinia Park.

This year's victory for the Eagles will alter the whole competition. It increases the prospect that in two or three years' time there will be a Fremantle as well as Perth team in the AFL. Twenty years from now there will probably be three W.A. teams and only nine Victorian teams in the Australian Football League.

IN OUR TIME

I think the day will come, maybe in 2007 when two W.A. teams play off in the Grand Final. Then Victorian supporters, as loyal as ever, won't know which team to boo.

It is hard to dispute this fact: Western Australia's population is likely to continue growing at a more rapid pace than Victoria. The "sandgropers" are already competitive and aggressive in many sports as well as in business. Their successes will multiply—unless Victoria and its economy both wake up.

Herald Sun, 28 September, 1992

When Football Was Just a Winter Game

The football season used to begin when the days were becoming cold and short. Cricket was well and truly finished before the first footballs were kicked about the parks. There was a time and place for everything, and the time for football was winter. Many barrackers would chop firewood in their back yard before walking to the grounds for the first match of the season.

In 1877, when Australian Rules was already the popular game in Victoria, the main teams did not play seriously until May was almost over. Thus, Carlton played its first game on 24 May when it journeyed to Ballarat, which in those days meant a long trip because the trains ran through north Geelong. A match so early in the season was usually called a "preliminary canter".

May was too early to risk the hard falls that, even then, were part of the game. In the years when few football grounds employed a groundsman and few grounds owned a garden hose, it made good sense to start the football season only after the earth had become soft. Too many players would have suffered broken limbs if football was played on the rock-hard grounds of March and April. The disadvantage of the late start to the football season was that by the end of May, the days were short. A match typically began at three o'clock and ended in dim light, with the crowd spilling on to the arena in the hope of seeing the players.

As football was soon attracting larger crowds than cricket, there was a temptation to bring forward the opening of the football season by a couple of weeks. It was not easy, however, to curtail cricket. Nearly all the football grounds were controlled by the cricket clubs, which preferred to retain the long cricket season. They simply said that cricket was for summer and football for winter.

Somehow the cricket season slowly became shorter. By 1914, the footballers had cribbed another month. That year, the football began on 18 April when the Victorian Football Association (which included three teams that are now in the league) kicked off. North Melbourne was at home to Brighton, Williamstown at home to Prahran, Port Melbourne to Northcote, and Brunswick to Footscray. In the other association match, Hawthorn played Essendon but that team was popularly called "Essendon Town" and normally played at Essendon, whereas the League Essendon played on the old East Melbourne cricket ground.

On the following Saturday, 25 April, 1914 (exactly a year before the landing at Gallipoli), the league played its opening matches, of which the first on the printed fixtures was South Melbourne versus the short-lived University club. A late start to the football season did not mean a late ending to the season. In that era the association tended to play its finals on the last four Saturdays of August, while the league played on the first four Saturdays of September.

The practice of beginning the Melbourne football season in the second half of April continued for another four or five decades. If Anzac Day fell on a Saturday — and football was not permitted on Anzac Day — a league team managed to fit in only one game by the end of April. Football remained a cold-weather game, and to hear for the first time the sound of a football being punted in the late afternoon was as symbolic as the first note of a thrush in spring.

We are creatures of habit, and everybody over the age of 30 probably takes a long time to become accustomed to this latest revolution in the seasons and the sight of footballers training through the summer and the night football beginning before the summer is over.

The lengthening of the season for all kinds of things is one of the profound social changes of the past 50 years. At one time, strawberries, green peas, tomatoes and a host of other foods could be bought only in a limited season; hot cross buns appeared only a few days before Easter; the great day for weddings was Easter Saturday; nobody swam in August; and few people went on holiday in the winter.

Technology, new fashions and commercial forces are standing tradition on its head. The time will come when serious football takes up nine or 10 months of the year. Children will then express surprise that football was once a winter game and that a match of the day often ended after sunset.

The Age, 3 April, 1993

IN OUR TIME

Ablett

He is the most memorable of footballers but in an odd way he is often hard to remember. There is something of the will of the wisp about Ablett. He is like a vanishing trick.

It is strange that one seems to remember more vividly other champions of Geelong. I seem to see old Reg Hickey, captain and coach in the late 1930s, occasionally wearing a sleeveless guernsey which was then uncommon, and slightly red in the face as he waits as full back beside the goalpost at the bay end of the Corio Oval. After 50 years still fresh in memory is wavy-haired Lindsay White, having led too far from goal, about to boot his long drop kick and sure to make the distance but not the six points. And Bob Davis, eternally running, is bouncing the ball with all the space in the world in front of him, running far faster than his bulky physique should have allowed.

For some reason my mind carries no set-picture of Gary Ablett. Is it because he is so unpredictable? Or so versatile? No specific skill is the essence or hallmark of his game, though his high marking, being so pictorial, receives the most attention on television and radio and the back page of the newspapers.

You could almost say that Ablett is a combination of certain of the great players of the recent past, born again in a new body. He is a long kick but adept at that gentle, almost soccer-like shot that is new to the game. Pitted against the high markers he can soar above them. He is a master of that last-second mark when the ball is just about to touch the ground. He is an exemplar of that last-minute shove in the back that used to be called illegal. He bumps with a crunch, like a barrel-chested ruckman. He is just as skilled as a small wingman in running at full pace and picking up a dribbling ball.

Few of us imagined that we would see in the one player that kind of low-slung brilliance of St Kilda's Darrell Baldock, the ball always on a string when near the grass, combined with the high marking of Essendon's John Coleman, the dodging of Les Foote at Arden Street, and the courage of Tony Shaw in grabbing a ball at the bottom of a pack. Ablett is every one of them, embodied in one pair of legs and arms.

He has off days, though on some of his ordinary days he performs at least one extraordinary feat. He plays so few bad games that they too are memorable. He had a woeful day against Melbourne on a warm day at the start of—was it the 1994 season? His performance in finals since the miraculous grand final against Hawthorn in 1989 has been patchy.

He was slightly out of touch during the grand final against the West Coast in 1994, a year in which he had risen to the heights. At the start of the next season maybe half of the football commentators did not pick Geelong to make the final eight, let alone the final two. Their pessimism must have stemmed from the instinct, which they wisely did not emphasise in public, that Ablett had well and truly passed his prime. And yet Geelong rose again in 1995, with Ablett playing uncannily week after week. Then came the grand final in which, to the dismay of so many, he was not himself. It is a sign of his almost divine status that supporters remain loyal to him.

His last three seasons have been astonishing for someone of his years. It is a feat to move to full forward - a graveyard for cunning, fading old champions transferred from down the field - and to shine there. Furthermore, to exceed 100 goals in each season and to earn enough kicks to have conceivably reached 150 goals - if he had been a straight-shooter - is one of the momentous feats in the history of the game. If the League were to award a Greater Brownlow for three successive years of rare achievement, he should win that medal.

He is unpredictable in so many ways. When he was approaching what seemed then to be the peak of his career, the Geelong club could not even feel sure whether he would bother to play any more games of football.

This casual characteristic is almost engaging - except to a coach. One day at Kardinia Park, I was fortunate to be invited into the players' room just before the game. There he was, merely pretending to do the warm-up exercises which all the other players were doing with gusto and vigour. He was not a team man until relatively late in his career. And yet his individualism, his lonely quality, his religious yearnings, command respect. They distinguish him.

Curiously, on the field he does not, until the moment he performs, look like *the champion*. If you were a foreign tourist in Geelong, and if you took a keen interest in a variety of sports, and if you were taken to your very first Australian football game, and if you were asked, just before the ball was bounced, which of the 36 players on the field was the acknowledged champion - no, you would probably not pick Gary Ablett. In days gone by, you might pick Jack Dyer or Ron Barassi after observing their visible presence and their commanding air when they ran on to the field. But unless you knew who Ablett was, would you pick him as the champion?

On the field he can be introspective and self-effacing. There is no swagger. At times he displays a lost-in-the-clouds look as if he does not know whether it is Saturday or Sunday. After he has brought down a remarkable mark, however, he is capable of breaking out into a slight smile of puzzlement or even of wonderment. It is a quarter smile, no more. It goes without saying that part of his extraordinary fame comes from television and the way the camera, more than ever before, captures in slow-motion his aerobatics and his facial expression.

He has given pleasure to enormous crowds: not universal pleasure because many supporters of opposing clubs wish he did not exist. It would be hard, however, to think of any other footballer of the last 60 years who has displayed so often his mixture of skill and magic along with a strand of humility and a strand of sheer aggression.

There have been miracle players in the past. Other miracle players will come again, once in a decade, once in a quarter century. It is futile to ask who is the best footballer of all time. We should simply marvel at this phenomenon, sometimes called 'the pontiff', while he is still around.

This essay was written as the final chapter or afterword of the pictorial book written by Ablett and called simply Gary Ablett. It was published by Pan Macmillan in August 1996.

IN OUR TIME

Shilling's Worth of Wisdom

At the top end of Bourke Street was a narrow-fronted shop presided over by Mrs Bird. A woman of personality and zest, with a capacity to convey the silent message that there would be no nonsense in her shop, she sold secondhand books. In the late 1940s, her shop could be crowded if six people arrived at once, for the gap between the high shelves on the wall and the space for browsers was narrow.

To tempt those students with little money, she would gather half a dozen odd books and tie them with string and label them at one shilling a bundle. It was no good saying to Mrs Bird that you wanted only one of the six. She was adamant that all must go: they were a family, not to be divorced. For some reason, she often included in her bundles the Bostonian classic by Oliver Wendell Holmes, *The Autocrat of the Breakfast Table*. As a casual attender at her shop, I was so put off by the book's persistent presence in her shilling bundles that I had a strong aversion to it until a few years ago when, by chance, I read a copy and found it full of wisdom and quiet humor in the 1857 style.

Mrs Bird's shelves sometimes concealed books that would now be called minor treasures. As a student, I paid two pounds (it might have been two guineas because Mrs Bird thought her better books deserved the dignity of guineas) for the leather-bound volumes of 1888, *Victoria and Its Metropolis*, and their hundreds of pages devoted to the strange biographies of a host of colonists who had made good in Victoria.

Evans' secondhand bookshop stood for many years in Swanston Street. Its staff looked slightly astonished when someone entered this quietest of shops with its sense of space that Mrs Bird could never emulate. There, in the 1950s, you could pick up, for a small sum, secondhand books autographed long ago by Henry Kendall, J. B. O'Hara, Richard Horne, Marie Pitt and other Australian writers.

The books once owned by Sir John Monash, the great soldier, could also be found. There was something exciting in casually picking up a book of no outward appeal and then discovering, from the inside cover, who had owned it.

In the secondhand bookshops of the 1940s and 1950s, books once owned by John Pascoe Fawkner could be bought for a song. Whether he was the founder of Melbourne does not greatly matter. He opened the first hotel and there he kept a library for his lodgers and wrote in longhand Melbourne's first newspaper. I'll never know what made me buy a book that I'm not likely to read, but I still own his two volumes, *Journals of an Embassy to the Court of Ava*, with his large signature scrawled with a fine nib and the blackest of ink across at least six separate pages of narrative. One of his signings comes as late as page 540. Presumably, Fawkner signed his name many times so that a lodger would think twice before stealing the book.

Once, in Kenneth Hince's bookshop, I picked up a smallish plum-colored book, printed in Ballarat in 1886 and called *Assiduity*. That noun, once so popular, is almost unused today. *Assiduity* was a long obituary of Richard Hart, President of the Australian Natives Association when it was becoming an eloquent voice calling for an Australian nation. Hart died young in the gold town of Stawell, when federation was still a dream. But when the Commonwealth was finally born in 1901, his earnest advocacy was remembered by Alfred Deakin, soon to become Prime Minister. Deakin, in his book *The Federal Story*, called Hart "a very Sir Galahad" who, in the course of his short life, fostered that "higher sentiment of duty" that did much to create our nation.

Finding it on the secondhand shelves, I was moved to see that this copy was presented to Deakin when he was a young Victorian politician. Just inside the book was a fading message written with a spidery hand when the book was hot from the press, and conveying to Deakin "kind regards from the parents of R. H. Hart. Stawell. July 26 1886".

One finds these nostalgic books infrequently, and then buys them only on a whim. They used to call it "touching the hem of a garment". Having bought them, one usually forgets them. No doubt a few such books were even hidden in Mrs Bird's one-shilling bundles, more than 40 years ago.

The Age, 3 July, 1993

IN OUR TIME

The Ascent of the Restaurant

The rise of the restaurant is one of the surprising events of the past 40 years. Nobody would have predicted that restaurants and cafés would appear in such huge numbers, gain such glamor, and cater for such a big section of the population.

For children who began school in my day, the café was virtually unknown. A country town might hold just one, and inside it a Greek wearing an apron usually presided. A typical family would never dream of having a meal in a café. For one thing, they couldn't afford it. For another, they probably did not think the cooking was better than "home-cooking", a phrase that carried a lot of glamor.

I can't remember eating a meal in a café until I was 17. A friend and I were hitchhiking to Mildura for the grape-picking, and the driver of the big furniture van stopped for breakfast in the main street of Wycheproof. In the café and milk bar, a few tables without a tablecloth were set aside for the steak and eggs, not forgetting the tomato and lettuce and beetroot that circled the plate. The food was first class if you were hungry.

The first time I ate exotic food was in Little Bourke Street in 1948. I guess there were fewer than 20 Chinese cafés in the whole of Melbourne and suburbs; and the Ling Nan, the simplest of places, was a great favorite. At peak hour, as soon as a table was empty and the spilled rice and soy sauce had been wiped away with a cloth (and the menu given a wipe for good measure), the table was occupied by eager newcomers.

On Saturday night, the customers did not dawdle in a café and sit and gossip after finishing their meal. They might just pause to roll a smoke or glance at the "stop press" of the evening paper before paying at the cash register.

The restaurants, and there were few even in the 1950s, were classier than cafés. Mr Dante Triaca's memorable No. 1 Swanston Street, approached by steep stairs at the side of Young and Jackson's, was one of the few restaurants in the heart of the city. Unlike a café, it was legally permitted to serve alcohol with meals but, after a certain hour, no more orders would be accepted by the waiter in the black tie. The Bring Your Own lay far into the future, as did the credit card.

All has changed. Melbourne's Yellow Pages carry more than 30 pages of restaurants. Even those restaurants beginning with the Italian and French words, La and Le, number some 50. Lygon Street alone has far more restaurants than the whole city held in the year of the first Holden.

The restaurant and café have become little Meccas of social life, partly because there is so much more spending money around — even in these leaner years. Families are smaller and that lowers the cost of eating out. Alcohol is more in fashion and diners dally over a glass and think nothing of a three-hour meal. And, of course, the sheer variety of restaurants means that people with money to spare can presumably eat out in a different restaurant every night of the year.

The popularity of restaurants also stems from a social fact. Whereas people used to dress up to go on the pictures on Saturday night or to church on Sunday, and there be on display, the restaurant — as *The Age Good Food Guide* makes clear — now is often a meeting place and social parade ground.

Some dining experts would argue that eating out on a large scale could not begin until the sheer variety of restaurants was multiplied. There is truth in this idea but most people earning good incomes in the 1930s would not have dined out even if Melbourne had another 100 exotic restaurants. To half of the population, a restaurant seemed slightly unwelcoming. It was "continental" and therefore to be treated warily.

Then the European-style restaurant would have had trouble in competing with home-cooking for the simple reason that the crowning glory of oldtime Australian wood-stove cooking was the pudding or sweet, now fallen from favor. What stylish European restaurant in Melbourne would have matched the golden syrup dumpling or Yorkshire pudding and lemon sauce, let alone offer a second helping free of charge?

The Age, 8 January, 1994

IN OUR TIME

Part 3
Themes of the 1990s

Listen to the Footsteps

Every year one of the most important collective decisions in Australia is made by people who move, who step somewhere else. We don't often discuss these movements of people and yet they have profound consequences. Even when we were passing through smooth economic times, the silent footsteps were intriguing. But the times are no longer smooth.

Since 1850 Australia has three times run up rather serious overseas debts. The two previous difficulties, in the early 1890s and the early 1930s, were much worse. But we have not yet emerged from our troubles, so a final comparison is premature. Indeed today's debt burden and Australia's lack of competitiveness are not yet being tackled and so they may well subdue us longer than is really necessary.

Flashback

It is salutary to look at the early 1890s for comparisons. Then, as now, Australia was much worse off than most other parts of the western world. Inside Australia, then as now, Victoria was the main sufferer. We are inclined, with casual confidence, to think that we are very unlikely to repeat the mistakes of the past. We say "it can't happen here". But it is happening here — the impossible is happening here.

Believe it or not, we are roughly following the path of the Victorians of a century ago. We know from recent experience the milestones of that slippery path. Heavy overseas borrowing, export income too low, a crisis in the balance of payments largely ignored, the State government living far beyond its means, pressures to pay debts becoming acute, some major financial institutions collapsing, the property market in a fainting fit, unemployment increasing. This gloomy succession of milestones was almost unimaginable 15 or 18 months ago. What is the next step along the path? It is probably loss of population from Victoria, maybe losses on a large scale.

A century ago, when Victoria was buffeted by financial failures, it lost population on a startling scale. Between 1891 and 1905 Victoria lost through net migration as many people as it had gained by net migration in the previous 30 years. I am simply pointing to what can happen when an economy is, as they say at the football, concussed.

During the depression of the 1890s, Melbourne's population was quickly passed and outstripped by Sydney. For some 70 years, every single census showed that New South Wales was growing faster than Victoria.

Then the tide was turned. From 1947 to 1954 Victoria, at last, grew more speedily in population than did NSW. In the next seven years — the early Bolte years — Victoria repeated the victory, its rate of growth exceeded only by South Australia's. Manufacturing was booming in Australia, and Melbourne was strong in factories. Moreover, the black coal of NSW was ceasing to be the turbine of the nation's economic progress, and the rising importance of brown coal and petroleum gave Victoria the break it had longed for. Victoria had another advantage. In those days most migrants came to Australia by sea, and they reached Port Melbourne before they reached Sydney, and in Melbourne most left the ship. To this day Melbourne remains the home of the main wave of emigration from continental Europe — the Baits and Germans, Dutch and Ukrainians, Italians and Maltese, Greeks and Yugoslavs.

In this astonishing post-war rejuvenation, Melbourne grew at a faster pace than Sydney in some 25 of the first 30 years. About 1976 Sydney finally grabbed, or re-grabbed, the ball. Once again it began to grow more rapidly than Melbourne. The high property prices of Sydney were one sign of its new victory.

The economic forces that had favoured Victoria subsided. Manufacturing became less important as a magnet for population; the European migration that had long favoured Melbourne was challenged by Asian, Middle Eastern, American and Pacific Island migrants, all of whom favoured Sydney. The haven for New Zealanders fleeing their own waterlogged ship was also Sydney. Since airways now surpassed the seaways as Australia's link with the world, and as Sydney was the main airport, it attracted the new finance houses that came to Australia. In tourism Sydney also outshone Melbourne. Sydney became the city of the Japanese yen; it was also the city of the American and Hong Kong and Singapore dollars and such Chinese money as was worth pocketing.

Sydney was now on rollerskates while Melbourne limped. Hardly a hint of this was aired in the Victorian State election campaigns of the 1980s. It is a sign of the weakness of Victoria's Opposition parties that they allowed Labor to boast about Victoria's impressive level of employment, and so win the economic debate. In fact, Victoria's unemployment was low in the 1980s partly because so many of the unemployed or the prematurely-retired Victorians went north to live.

Unemployment was low partly because the Government, without counting the cost, was employing more and more people in the public sector. A key fact did not even enter the debate, namely that in the years 1976 to 1986 Victoria and Tasmania tied for the booby prize as the states growing most slowly in population.

Admittedly, in the last two years, Victoria has grown more rapidly than New South Wales in population. That is a temporary revival. The most likely cause is that the Greiner Government boldly began to do what the Cain Government failed to do: pruned a lot of the dead wood from the public sector and especially the railways. In other words, Victoria is already vulnerable, without the present bad news.

Australians' Sun Hat

Part of the challenge to Victoria, and to New South Wales too, comes from far away. It comes from the big warm outer States and Territories. They are experiencing one of the most remarkable population shifts in Australian history. If it continues at the same pace as in the last 30 years its implications will be profound.

In the days of the Model-T Ford some observers used to say that Queensland and Western Australia had our future in their hands. They were called "the coming states" because they had a vast area and untapped resources. They were always coming but never quite arriving. Even in the 1950s when Arthur Fadden was Treasurer, they did not show the steady pace of growth they have since displayed. The census of 1961 revealed that Queensland's population had been growing at only the national average, while Western Australia was below the national average. Then came the 1966 census, the Harold Holt census if you like. In rate of growth Western Australia was suddenly on top, having jumped from fourth to first, while Queensland was third. Then came the 1971 census, the Billy McMahon census. Western Australia and Queensland were on top. They have remained the pacemakers ever since. This year's census will show them still on top.

For the last 20 years, Western Australia and Queensland have in aggregate been increasing their population at twice the percentage of NSW and Victoria combined. There is no real sign that the pacemakers are tiring. In the year ending June 1989 the two big outer States were growing at nearly three times the pace of Victoria and NSW. In certain years of the later 1980s, Perth and Brisbane each grew at nearly four times the pace of Melbourne.

Will this Sun Hat of the Australian continent continue to grow far more rapidly than the old power base? We used to believe that the mineral boom was the main cause of their growth. And yet WA and Queensland continued to outstrip the rest of Australia even in the 1980s when minerals and other primary industries were no longer the dynamo of growth.

A preference for a warm climate is one ingredient of the economic success of the Sun Hat of Australia. In the United States, the dramatic rise of California, Florida and Texas mirrors the power of the new sunbelt. Leisure now challenges work as a determinant of where people settle. The growing number of retired people and the ease of air travel partly explain the popularity of Queensland with its thousand-mile tourist coast.

In the year ending June 1990, Queensland gained more people through interstate migration than it gained from all other causes — namely natural increase and immigration from overseas. Queensland's rate of increase from interstate migration alone exceeded NSW's rate of increase from all sources combined. New South Wales, especially Sydney, is the diligent supplier of settlers to Queensland — Victoria had been in the mid-1980s. Sydney is passing into an unusual stage: it is now the mecca for overseas migrants but the source of the great exodus of Australian-born people. Ethnically it is likely to become Australia's New York.

Western Australia is the other large gainer from interstate migration. If WA were not isolated I am sure it would compete with Queensland as the mecca for those dissatisfied with where they live. Cheap air fares could make Perth more a magnet. But it still cannot compete with Queensland in tourism.

I am tempted to include the Northern Territory with the big outer States. It shares their geographical characteristics and their special interests. It is different in this respect: that it has few people and they depend far more than WA and Queensland on Federal funds. The Northern Territory is a kind of single-mother living mainly on subsidies. Darwin is in many ways a tropical clone of Canberra, a public-service town. With the locking up of so much of the Northern Territory resources because of Aboriginals', conservationists' and anti-uranium claims, and with some restraint on the Federal budget in recent years, the Northern Territory has recently ceased to gallop ahead in population. In the last three years (July 1987 to June 1990) the Northern Territory has become, in its rate of population growth, the snail of Australia. Even Tasmania has performed more impressively.

The New Map for Australia?

What if Queensland, Western Australia and the Northern Territory continue to grow faster than the rest of Australia by the same margin as in the recent decades? Today they hold about 27.5 per cent of Australia's population. By the year 2050, if the present trend continues, they will have about 45 per cent of Australia's population. In short, the six-year-olds now at school will, in the year of their retirement, see some 45 per cent of Australia's population living in the big outback States and Territories. Now I am not positively predicting that in the next 60 odd years this will happen. I am simply saying that if Australia continues to experience the pattern of population growth of the last 30 years, it will need new economic and political maps.

It would be a very different Australia if the big outer states formed a counter-balance to the south-east corner. After all, these outer states tend to have different priorities and attitudes: traditionally they take defence more seriously, they have a different perspective on Aboriginal issues, they are more conscious of the closeness of Asia, they are slightly less interested than the south-east corner in big government, slightly more suspicious of Canberra. Moreover, their economic impetus stems more from natural resources. If these big outer states continued to grow, the Labor-Liberal rivalry could cease to be the dominant contest of national politics and could be rivalled by the contest between the south-east corner and the rest of Australia. In several topics this conflict has already happened. The momentum of Aboriginal land rights came to a halt about 1986 when Western Australia (a Labor Government, mind you) rebelled against the generosity of the south-east corner in giving northern and western land to Aborigines.

In the long-term, the swing of population towards the big, warm, outer states could well be in Australia's interests and therefore indirectly in the interests of all Victorians. Meanwhile, Victoria has to face its own economic difficulties. It has performed poorly since about 1975 in attracting and retaining people. It has performed poorly despite — perhaps because of — the huge injection of money into job creation. The bad news of the last nine months can only aggravate Victoria's plight. We should hear the footsteps.

And yet there is wide, wide scope for optimism in Victoria. With thought and effort, Victoria could dramatically improve its waterfront, its railways, and the public transport in the cities. With commonsense it could transform its education system (if you can use the word "system" instead of subsidized chaos). With effort and imagination Victoria could transform its tourism, one of its grave weaknesses. With deft lobbying in this new era of privatization it could challenge the way Qantas has helped make Sydney the international airport. By taking thought it could smarten up what is left of its manufacturing industry, and with some flair and drive it could even compete with New Zealand in supplying packaged fruit and vegetables to South-East Asia.

With determination, Victorians could also make the massive state bureaucracy less costly and less massive; with forethought they could work towards eliminating the incredible duplication and overlap of Federal, State and Local Government services in the same field. And these are only the beginnings. With such changes, Victorians would give all Australians a lead in making the nation more competitive. With such opportunities, who can be pessimistic?

IPA Review, 1991

The Gulf War and the Peace Crusade

The place of the peace movement

If the war in the Persian Gulf should last one, two or three years, the opposition inside Australia to that war could become very disruptive, with tactics unlike those used against the Vietnam War.

Prime Minister Bob Hawke had one eye on stemming that when he promised that Australia would not increase its forces in the Gulf. That promise he will probably have to break if the war is longer and more difficult than he expects. Some opposition, however, will not be curbed easily because it reflects ideologies positively fostered by his party in the belief – strong in the second half of the '80s – that Australia would never find itself in the situation it now faces.

The rickety discipline of peace studies had been encouraged in schools by Labor Ministers in Canberra and the states in the belief that it would generate the kind of anti-war opposition visible throughout the country. Senior Labor leaders did not envisage that this ideology would turn against them. The environmental movement had also been favoured by Hawke. In opposing the war, it is carrying out an ideology which this time last year Hawke seemed to bless with subsidies, election-eve speeches and a promise of "absolute commitment".

His party can no longer offer sanctuary to ardent advocates of peace. At the outbreak of World War II, however, it contained a strong "peace" movement made up of competing – even conflicting – strands. Some of Labor's peace advocates were primarily nationalist and isolationist; some were internationalist and friendly with Moscow and some were old-time pacifists and gallant, wartime stretcher-bearers. Others marched two steps behind the main peace movement, ready to join it if their special hatred – the conscription of Australians for overseas service – were tried again.

John Curtin, Labor's leader in 1939, had half of his heart in that peace movement. Even in 1940 – a year before he became Prime Minister – he was sympathetic to the idea of tentative peace negotiations with Hitler. That movement initially had more influence, at the outbreak of war in September 1939, than the modern peace movement has. The movement of 1939 was hit hard when the Soviet Union, invaded by Hitler in June 1941, became a war movement when, six months later, Japan threatened Australia's security.

Generally, an anti-war movement can flourish only while the war is very costly and is made to seem irrelevant ot our security. For those reasons the movement grew as the Vietnam War went on and on. At present a minority movement, it will expand if this war goes on and on and if the sphere of fighting remains far from our shores.

Labor's links with the peace movement of 1991 are tangled. Demanding the instant withdrawal of Australian vessels from the Gulf, a group of Labor women in Queensland last week said they were invoking a proud Labor tradition. It is hardly a tradition. But a definite Labor tradition – and an aid to peace elements within its ranks – is that Labor had never been in power when Australia made its previous decisions to enter a major war. For the first time a Labor government has made the decision, one which will have profound consequences for the peace movement and the party.

If the Liberals were in office and a Liberal government had made the decision to send warships, the Labor Party would be more divided in its attitude to the war. Some of Hawke's present Ministers, if in opposition, would have opposed the war. Moreover, the party would have more easily accommodated its anti-war elements. But Labor has courageously made its stand and it cannot remain, as in other wars, the main party of protest. The Democrats have usurped that role. In Federal Parliament they lack the numbers and seem to lack the talent to play it well. Therefore, the peace movement – unless Labor splits – will largely be centred outside Parliament. Such an anti-war movement is less likely to be orthodox in its tactics.

Spectators in Parliament House last month interrupted a debate on the question of whether the nation should have gone to war. This gang, in the name of peace, violated the process of free discussion which all genuine advocates of peace would see as sacred. That the Parliamentarians were so patient is to their credit. It might have seemed vindictive if they had reacted sternly. Sadly, the leaders of the peace movement did not promptly disown their wilder supporters. Presumably, other acts of political thuggery can be expected.

Some danger of a split in the Labor Party must remain. It has tended to experience its disastrous splits when in power; moreover, the divisive issue has always had an international component and twice a military one. The causes of two main splits were military conscription during World War I and the threat of international communism in 1955 during the Cold War.

Hawke, with a legitimate claim to the title of the best political general in the history of the party, will be alert to the danger of a serious split. He also knows that hostility to his war plans will increase in the more militant trade unions just when their support is vital for work-practice reform. If the war were to continue for the remaining two years of his term of office, his chances of reshaping the economy must be judged not small but minute. Even his chance of greatly increasing Australia's contribution to the war effort in the Middle East is dubious.

These conclusions are suggested by the present state of the war on the one hand and the state of his Labor Party opponents on the other. However, an unpredictable turn of events in the war or at home could keep public opinion strongly on his side.

The environmental movement is the hub of the peace crusade, a fact inconceivable 30 years ago. Opinion polls also show that the peace movement depends more on women's sympathies than on men's. Much of its support comes from the young. The movement has other supporters it could not have enlisted in any previous war. It has a big number of Islamic sympathisers. It also has Iraqi supporters – as well as opponents – though Iraq is only a tiny source of Australian migrants. Many of these peace-people are not only Australian citizens but also remain citizens of their homeland. New Australian citizens no longer have to renounce their old allegiances. The current rhetoric insists that they are as loyal as any other Australians. Most presumably are loyal, despite the conflicting calls on their affections. Some are unbelievably loyal. Others feel the tension acutely, especially if they have at least one ear open to Saddam Hussein's talk of a holy war.

All citizens are entitled to express views for or against Australia's role. But that statement hardly makes the position easy for Arab Moslems who feel intensely about this issue but live and work among non-Moslems, many of whom feel intensely in a different way.

Politicians of both sides – but especially Labor – have urged ethnic groups to maintain their culture and view of the world, to maintain homeland ties and therefore many of their loyalties, to speak with one voice through their official spokespeople, to stand together and therefore to stand apart to some degree from the society that has generously given them citizenship.

In view of that long-standing official attitude, what are besieged ethnic groups to do now? Are they to state their views and risk accusations of disloyalty to Australia's official policy or are they to sit in angry silence? Official policy, in failing to see how easily this dilemma could arise, should be carefully examined when this war is over.

High casualties and threats to the environment could quickly spur opposition. The alarming spill of oil was a fillip to the anti-war movement but part of that came from a lack of perspective. The oily sea along part of the Gulf was widely depicted as potentially "the worst ecological disaster zone in history". Such statements are nonsense, ignoring the larger catastrophes stemming over thousands of years from nature itself.

The peace movement is also aided by a belief that the world is too small for military pranks and that the billions spent on the missiles could transform the health of much of the Third World. Professor Fred Hollows, named Australian of the Year for his great work with the Aborigines, emphasised the internationalist view last month when he argued that Australia should not be fighting the Gulf War.

"Patriotism, as you know, is the last resort of scoundrels," he added. Obviously he has not seen the origins of that celebrated quotation in Boswell's *Life of Johnson*. Johnson admired genuine patriotism.

Internationalism can equally be the last resort of scoundrels. Many supporters of peace demand an end to some wars but not others. While a host of them are people of goodwill, earnest hopers for peace, others are primarily anti-American, anti-capitalist, anti-military, anti-technology, anti-oil or anti-this-and-that rather than positively dedicated to peace. Peace is written on their banner but the small print is more revealing. Even if a peace movement is dominated by saints and idealists, it is not necessarily working for peace.

War is one of the most unpredictable of all human activities. A frequent mistake of national leaders is to believe that their brand-new war will be short and victorious. One frequent mistake of the advocates of peace is to believe that their efforts will surely lead to peace and that the peace will be long and glorious.

Hitler had reason to be grateful to the peace movement in Europe. He could not have re-armed in the mid-'30s without its unwitting help. The governments of France and England, if public opinion had been strongly behind them, could have squashed Hitler with little loss of life in 1936. The peace movement was one loud voice calling for "no action". It succeeded, thus paving the way for the most terrible war.

The peace movement has to be taken seriously. It represents an important cluster of viewpoints. But it should not always be taken seriously. At times it can promote war. Or the peace it assists in imposing on a nation or a part of the world can turn out to be tyrannical and murderous for people living under it.

Advocates of war face the same danger. A war begun with too much optimism or a war whose aims become increasingly ambitious can be many times deadlier and costlier than originally anticipated, thus providing legitimate scope for a peace movement to call "enough".

The Bulletin, 12 February, 1991

IN OUR TIME

The Plight of the Factory

It is not surprising that Australia's manufacturing industry has declined in the last 20 years. What is surprising is the ignorance of the consequences awaiting the nation if the decline is allowed to go too far.

The basic problem facing a wide range of surviving Australian factories and workshops is the nation and the national culture they are operating in. If many of these factories could be lifted up and taken to east Asia, they would soon become competitive.

These factories would be transformed not by cheap labour but by incentives to invest in new plant, by lower taxation and more predictable government policies. Curiously, the Federal Government's new policy on manufacturing gives them every incentive to go offshore and send their goods back to Australia.

For a debt-burdened nation needing fewer imports the policy is doubly strange. Canberra's policy of reducing the tariffs on imported manufactures might make good sense in prosperous years but today, with our towering overseas debts, it makes little sense.

To destroy or close down too many factories as part of the alleged process of rejuvenating Australia's economy is to kill the baby on the grounds that the humidicrib needs to be rebuilt.

Australia has seen several revolutions in attitudes to the manufacturing industry. But in the first phase of what appears to be another revolution, we should look carefully at the likely effects. The latest long-term policy, proclaimed by Mr Hawke in March 1991, is not likely to work.

For a long time the manufacturer was almost a patron saint of this nation. H.V. McKay and his Sunshine harvester, Barnet Glass and his "boomerang" tyre, the Mephan Fergusons and the Hoskins and Humes and their cast-iron and steel and concrete pipes - they were household names. Most Australians were proud of their factories and the machines in them.

Part of the respect for factories was that they provided jobs when farms and mines could no longer provide them. Factories surpassed farms as an employer of labour in the 1920s and kept on growing. Every state premier, every lord mayor, would do almost anything to attract a new factory to his domain (so long as it did not select his own residential suburb).

By 1939, on the eve of war, Australia was probably more important in world manufacturing than it is today. For a nation of seven million people it was perhaps attempting too much.

The war with Japan was a further spur to manufacturing. Australia's policy in the following two decades was to foster every kind of factory, refinery and smelter in the hope that the nation would become self-sufficient.

The Snowy Mountains Scheme was launched as much to foster factories as to promote irrigated-farm products. As Mr Chifley's Minister, Nelson Lemmon, told the Federal Parliament in 1949, the Snowy's cheap electricity would boost "the industrial effort of our nation should Australia be faced with the threat of war". The tariff gave help to virtually every factory that wanted it. The import restrictions imposed during the 1950s in order to ease the adverse balance of payments were a further solace to manufacturers.

Many of their industries were too protected, and yet the productivity in most factories improved rapidly. In the 19 years from June 1949 the output for each factory employee rose at an annual 4.1 per cent, which was even more than in farming. While Mr Hawke and Mr Keating say they are now repairing the disgraceful inefficiency inherited from the 1950s and 1960s, they are really blaming the past as an excuse for their own neglect.

The nation's policy on manufacturing in the time of Curtin, Chifley and Menzies was based on the needs of the economy and national defence, and has to be judged as such. By the late 1960s, however, the defence argument was weakened.

The strength of the alliance with the US meant that Australia was less likely to be a source of arms, munitions, aircraft and machine tools in the event of war. The old argument for a strong manufacturing industry as a buttress in wartime virtually slipped from national thinking, though it was voiced, curiously, as late as 1983 in Mr Hawke's first election speech when he promised to "rebuild our manufacturing base" and make factories again central to the nation's security.

Manufacturing had also been seen as a vital provider of jobs, and in the Chifley-Menzies years the job argument and the defence argument marched to the same tune. In the big immigration program after World War II, floods of new jobs were needed. The factories supplied them.

Full employment was hailed as the post-war miracle, and R.G. Menzies nearly lost the Federal election of 1961 because the level of unemployment, which was edging past two per cent, aroused fears of a return to the bread-and-dripping years. In such a mood, the continuing ability of factories to provide jobs was all-important.

Then in the late 1960s and the 1970s, manufacturing lost some of its glamour. The mineral boom encouraged us to do those things in which we were most competitive. So we exported more minerals and, in exchange, imported more manufactured goods.

At the same time, new Asian factories were now outselling Detroit, Birmingham, and the smokestack cities of the old world. If Detroit could not compete with east Asia, what hope had Botany, Woodville and Dandenong?

Canberra understandably abandoned the idea of a self-sufficient Australia. Under Mr Whitlam the tariff on foreign manufactures was cut. In his first exuberant year he cut import duties by a heavy 25 per cent. He must have made earlier Labor politicians turn in their grave - or turn in their coffins of all-Australian manufacture.

The woes of Australian factories were increased by the fact that in a few months the currency was revalued by about 18 per cent - so favourable was the balance of payments.

There followed a quick decline in the national role of the factory. In Victoria, the heartland of factories, the total of factory employees fell by a sixth in the space of a few years. Between 1973, the first year of Mr Whitlam, and 1983, when Mr Fraser was defeated, there was an upheaval in manufacturing. Its proportion of the Australian workforce fell from 28 to 18 per cent. Not even farming, in its relative decline as an employer, had been buffeted so quickly.

Export incentives, John McEwen's golden syrup, also vanished. From the mid-1970s the bipartisan change of policy spurred some Australian factories to move offshore.

One of the departures was Ansell, which some would say is about the most competitive Australian manufacturer there has ever been. It began moving from the Yarra bank at Richmond to Malaysia and then to other lands where it became world leader in such booming latex products as surgical gloves, industrial gloves and condoms. To step offshore was a response by some Australian manufacturers that believed in themselves but did not believe in Canberra.

The decline of immigration in the 1970s was partly a result of the end of the boom in Australian factories and their waning hunger for labour. In contrast, the vigorous revival of immigration in the mid-1980s was not really linked to economic policy, whether manufacturing or resources or service industries. It is a sign of Canberra's tendency to ignore economic realities that its leaders began to boast to the world that in many Australian factories about 40 different nationalities worked side by side. Ironically a factory with language barriers was less efficient; but efficient was hardly in Canberra's vocabulary.

The Hawke Government for most of its years was, verbally, positive towards manufacturing. Senator Button tried to help industry, but some of his colleagues unconsciously worked in the opposite direction.

For six Hawke years the investment growth in new plant, in real terms, ran at a pleasing nine per cent a year. Then investment slowed down alarmingly in nearly every sector of economic life. Overall, the proportion of the workforce in manufacturing did not decline in Mr Hawke's heyday.

Australia, through its poor economic performance relative to its neighbours, was no longer such a dear-labour land. Canberra did not proclaim that "achievement".

Alongside the slow decline in many Australian secondary industries was an expansion in others. Exports of manufactured goods became important, though a lot of the increase was to New Zealand and Papua New Guinea. Aluminium and steel exports were a success story but some gains were in the automotive and other industries which did not depend on Australian resources. Government incentives played a part in this export surge.

Such was the optimism that in March 1990 Mr Keating said that Australia would soar out of its economic difficulties, as if carried along in the jetstream of manufactured exports. In extolling manufacturing, he spoke of an export-led recovery of such vigour that Australia before long could dispense with its old outback exports and revel in the intricate whizzbang of the 21st century. His preposterous prediction received little criticism.

Too many statements about economic policy in Australia are not statements but outbursts. They are designed to meet a temporary political need.

Exactly one year later, Mr Hawke, in his long-heralded "industry statement", shunned Mr Keating's optimism. He said Australia was still so uncompetitive that stern measures were needed. He declared war on tariffs. By 2000 even the tariff on motor vehicles would be down to 15 per cent. And that would be one of the higher tariffs, one of the few stretches of the tariff wall that was more than ankle-high.

Mr Hawke saw a vital but humbler place for manufactured exports: "Our rural and mineral products will remain important into the future. But the challenge is to add to them. That is, we must export more manufactured goods and services and substitute more quality Australian production for imports."

If this is the aim, why is the Government at this stage removing the benefits from factories before it removes the numerous obstacles? Its policy reads like a replay of Whitlam—except that Whitlam acted when the balance of trade was wonderfully in Australia's favour and the nation had little overseas debt.

Local factories competing against cheap imports are likely to close long before the factories striving for exports take up the leeway, if ever they do. This means that imports will pour in—the very event Australia must avoid if the balance of payments is to be tackled.

Difficult changes, whether in the labour market or the taxing of depreciation, are needed before local industries are fit to meet stronger competition from imports. Moreover, there is only one permanent way in which many Australian factories can compete. They must spend heavily on the best machinery, operate it for as many as 150 hours a week, and employ the minimum of labour.

The minimum of labour - that is often the key. The traditional idea of seeing factories primarily as a solver of unemployment now has knobs on it. That fallacy is being revived in every Parliament house, but unemployment should be seen as the number two enemy. If we could only fight the abject state of the balance of payments we would begin to solve the unemployment problem, solving it indirectly.

We need the latest labour-saving machines but Canberra's tax laws discourage factories from buying them. In January this year an OECD study revealed that in its 24 member countries, Australia did the most to dissuade manufacturers from buying new plant, machinery and equipment.

Such a contrast mocks Canberra's confident talk about our move towards a "level playing field". The phrase is a substitute for thought and a pretext for not observing what other nations do.

This sporting analogy about a playing field should be rewritten in this way: In the 1960s Canberra probably became too eager to provide a home-ground advantage for manufacturers. But now Canberra is going too far to remove the home-ground advantage at the very time when it is urgently needed.

The Plight of the Factory

In the next few years we have to prevent imports - and the overseas debts they incur - from growing at more than a snail's pace. Therefore we can't afford to allow manufacturing to decline. Otherwise, when the economy starts to pick up, as it assuredly will, the wharves and the airport sheds will be jammed with imports of manufactures, many of which we once made here. With the flood of imports the debt will be even more out of control, thus preventing us from moving to the next stage of economic recovery.

In the last depression, 60 years ago, Australia gave strenuous aid to manufacturing. That helped the nation to recover. That policy also tackled a balance of payments that was as perturbing as it is today. Admittedly it would now be foolish to protect factories to anything like the same degree that we did then, or we will end up with too many inefficient industries. But to go out of our way to endanger manufacturing in the middle of a depression is to be dumb.

The valuable report on manufacturing written in 1990 by Pappas, Carter, Evans and Koop argued that in a global economy the old policy of protection does not work. They also gave this warning: "to expose firms that were nurtured in protected times to open competition, especially abruptly, is likely to lead more often to their closure than to their transformation into vigorous world-beaters." For Canberra to offer a host of factories to the wolves is to ignore the intensity and aggression of some of the overseas competition.

At least Canberra is right to say that manufacturing is a game in which Australians must become more competitive. But the game is often played not on a grassy playing field but in a jungle. In that jungle the Government now behaves like an inexperienced cub.

Australian Business Monthly, March 1992

IN OUR TIME

Cyclone Keating

Since the birth of the Commonwealth, only six Federal politicians – by my count – have been able to stamp their signature decisively and almost continuously on a particular decade. To have spent about nine years of a 10-year period as Prime Minister, Deputy Prime Minister or Treasurer is a feat surpassed by Sir Robert Menzies, Sir John McEwen, and equalled only by Sir Arthur Fadden, Harold Holt, Bob Hawke and Paul Keating.

Although most of the past 10 years were primarily Hawke years, Mr Keating often let it be known that he was really running the country. It would be unfair to take him at his own word and blame him exclusively for those economic policies that failed. Moreover, he can't be blamed for the arrival of a world slump, though he did a lot to throw us into deep water before the slump reached these shores.

The Keating-Hawke period is one of the stark economic disappointments in Australia's past 150 years. That era began with an air of competence and confidence, saw some useful and a few brave changes, but Australia was eventually left far behind by faster changes in the outside world and by mistakes and inertia, public and private, at home.

Our standing on the world's economic ladder has slipped. In the era of Chifley and Menzies (1945-66), the rate of unemployment was always much lower in Australia than in the US. In the years when Paul Keating was Treasurer, the unemployment here was nearly always worse than in the US. It still is decidedly worse.

Often in the past decade, Australia's inflation rate ran far above that of its main competitors. The Keating formula tended to price us out of export markets and to escort foreign imports into our own supermarkets. His job-creation schemes of the 1980s owed much to the debt-creation he presided over. Now even the Keating jobs have mostly vanished. Likewise, the Australian dollar is the crowned dunce of the currencies of the OECD nations, having fallen even more than the British pound and Italian lira.

In defending his record, Keating is full of fight. While reading a set speech he might be a little stilted, but off the cuff he can be masterly. Now he is exuberantly and aggressively Australian in almost everything he says, though five years ago he wanted more the approval of New York than Bankstown. His verbal skills, however, have become his enemy. His forté is to toss tasty morsels to the cameras night after night but some of the morsels are now stuck on his own face.

He has been allowed to outlive a procession of extraordinary and misguided statements and many major mistakes of policy. Month after month he predicted that the J curve would curb our overseas debts. When no curve appeared, he promised a hundred times in 1986 and 1987 that his new policy would reduce our overseas debts, but, alas, they have continued to soar.

Three years ago, Mr Keating poured contempt on those who said the overseas debts might badly hurt the average Australian. Partly through his negligence, these debts, rising every month, could well blow out during the first phase of the economic recovery, preventing Australia from full recovery.

He is still accorded rather a lot of credibility by part of the Canberra media that helped him to oust Bob Hawke — after the electorate had voted for Hawke. Surprisingly, he is making some headway with his attacks on the likely effect of the goods and services tax. This Treasurer, who bit by bit raised the income tax on the average Australian's salary to a record percentage, is now allowed to pose as the sworn enemy of taxation changes.

Since he became Treasurer in 1983, the cumulative rise in the CPI is more than 75 per cent; and part of this inflation came from his policies. But now he is mightily indignant at the thought of a GST, which, after removing a few taxes, would probably raise average prices by only three or four per cent in the first crucial year.

His annual budget statements from 1983 to 1990 should be printed on silk for people to keep, reminding them of how often a Treasurer can make wrong but electorally attractive promises about inflation, unemployment, overseas debts and taxation. Like a tropical cyclone, he remains hyperactive and highly news-worthy. Nobody can tell the course that Cyclone Keating will take, but the damage that follows in his wake is perhaps easier to predict.

The Age, 6 March, 1993

IN OUR TIME

Royal Ambitions

The prevailing view is that the push to make Australia a republic will grow stronger each year, achieving the easiest of victories. In Sydney—the heart and voice of the republican movement—several newspapers carry the proposition that the push could succeed this year if Mr Keating decided to press his luck. I doubt whether the republicans will have a dream run. Long patches of ankle-deep mud lie ahead of them. A defeat in 2001, their proposed year of triumph, is still feasible.

One of the most remarkable political campaigns of recent times, the crusade for a republic relies partly on public ignorance. Australia's political system is complicated and there can be no doubt that the role of the monarch is the crowning complication. A big minority of Australians, and especially those who have arrived here in recent times, believe that the monarch is still a powerful figure in Australia with a mysterious right to influence Australian affairs. In fact, the Queen would quickly cease to be Queen of Australia if she were seen to be interfering in Australian affairs. By the political definitions of 1900 — or even 1945 — Australia is already a republic.

At the same time, the rising tide against the monarchy is beyond dispute. The monarch's role and power in Australia are more fragile than in the United Kingdom, and even there the royal antics, reported or inferred, have done immense harm, though not necessarily long-term harm, to the monarchy. In Australia, the polls show a strong shift towards a republic, though some of the polls have to be read with a grain of salt. The most publicised poll, with strong republican results, actually asked a sample of Australians whom they would prefer as "head of state". As most of us never use the term "head of state" in any kind of conversation, such an opinion poll is not as credible as it has been proclaimed. In any case, to ask people what they think of the present system of government is very different to asking them what they will think of a new republican package in which the power of Mr Keating might be very much increased.

Mr Keating initially announced that he would appoint a committee of eminent persons to advise on what kind of republic Australia should become. No doubt many of the people he appoints will be eminent, though not in the matter under discussion. Moreover, as a group, they will be pre-eminent primarily for their political predictability. And if by chance their formula disappoints Mr Keating, then he will probably declare that they were not as eminent as he had first thought and amend or discard their recommendations. The eminent persons are hostages to Mr Keating's own political shrewdness.

His present position on the republic is not defensible. He insists that the monarchy must disappear but he does not indicate which of the many alternatives should replace it. For him to be more definite would perhaps disclose his hand and also divide the united republican movement.

Mr Keating is emphatic that any alternative system would be better than the present. He is uneasy with the checks and balances that provide one of the strengths of our sort of government. Given his distaste for the monarchy, given his distaste for the Senate, and given his distaste for the previous rival in his own party and for the leader of the opposition (whoever that might be), he is not likely to propose a republican system in which the present office of Prime Minister loses even a stitch of power. Would Mr Keating support a republic in which the Governor-General, no matter what he is called, retains even his present role of sorting out the constitutional crises that will occasionally arise?

The present system of government, for all its faults, has great merits, not least being its checks and balances. Mr Keating's ideal seems to be a system in which the Queen is displaced, the Governor-General has less political power than at present, the Senate is cut down to size, and question time in the House of Representatives — that vital check — is sometimes turned into a political zoo. In Mr Keating's view, the states themselves should also have less power. All this would render Canberra and the reigning Prime Minister more powerful than ever before. Is this ardent opponent of the last vestiges of the monarchy really — at heart — an ambitious monarch?

The Age, 17 April, 1993

IN OUR TIME

Aborigines' Losses and Gains

It seems hard to debate Mabo and the rights of living Aborigines without comparing the way of life of old-time Aborigines and the life of recent Australians. Land rights are seen by many, including, to some extent, the High Court, as a form of compensation for what Aborigines have lost. If this is so, then the extent of Aborigines' losses since 1788 becomes a way of determining the compensation.

I'm not sure how far it is sensible to see land rights for Aborigines as the equivalent of "damages" in a court case but the comparison between Australia before 1788 and the same land a century or two later will continue to be made. It is not easy to do it fairly. Moreover, the knowledge of how Aborigines lived 200 or 2000 years ago is punctured with holes.

A strong case can be made that the Aborigines were successful if measured by the times in which they lived. For example, it is often said that they lived in harmony with their natural environment and had an expert knowledge of the seasons, the plants and animals. This is beyond dispute but the case can't be carried too far.

Aborigines did change and harm the environment. Fire was their special weapon and many botanists argue that Aborigines, by constant burning, created the grasslands of south-eastern Australia. They also extinguished species, some of them remarkable: the grazing diprotodon, giant kangaroos and, almost, the "Tasmanian Tiger" which once flourished on this continent but, by 1788, was confined to Tasmania. We newcomers finished off the Tasmanian rarity and many others.

On the score of the environment, the Aborigines were the winners. So long as their population remained relatively low, they also enjoyed a reasonable standard of living. My own view is that, in 1788, they had a more varied and balanced diet and less vulnerability to famine than, say,

80 per cent of the people of Europe. The great advance in Western standards of living has come in the past 200 years.

On various other grounds, the Aborigines were slightly or substantially worse off. At the same time, it is unwise to despise their society. It probably was rich in leisure, which, after all, has become one of the goals of Western civilisation. Its people were all-rounders rather than specialists and that was probably a source of contentment. Moreover, a mighty lot of ingenuity was built into their way of life.

There is a catch in trying to work out what the Aborigines lost when the Europeans arrived and, thereby, trying to calculate what modern sum in "damages" or compensation should be paid to their survivors. What happened to the Aborigines after 1788 had probably happened a few thousand years earlier to all our ancestors, whether they lived on the northern plains of Europe, the coasts of east Asia or an island in the Mediterranean. All over the world, the relatively simple way of life of hunters and gatherers was wrecked by the coming of people who domesticated plants and animals. A new economy arose, a new way of holding and working land arose and, everywhere, groups of people lost their vast sweeps of land and became the possessors—if they owned anything—of tiny areas of land.

Put it another way: in the pre-Christian era, the food supply of the world and the total population of the world probably increased dramatically with the invention of agriculture and gardens and the keeping of flocks and herds. As a result, each person's average share of the total land in the region they inhabited diminished rapidly, diminishing bit by bit over hundreds of years, and probably without any compensation being paid.

The living Aborigines, especially those in the outback, are possibly being treated with high generosity by the standards of most of our ancestors who suffered some 5000 years ago. Moreover, the land now handed or returned to the Aborigines is far, far more valuable than when they lost it. Its value has risen because of the application of science and technology and the sheer multiplication of the world's population.

On the other hand, many Aborigines, glimpsing the way of life their ancestors have lost, and knowing the sadness and bewilderment of it all, think no compensation is adequate. In one sense, they are right, though their way of life was bound to be overthrown eventually, because it supported so few people on so much land.

The Age, 31 July, 1993

IN OUR TIME

Didgeridoo and Kanguru

The Federal Government, while throbbing with fatherly goodwill towards Aborigines, is fundamentally defeatist. It does not dare say so but it seems to believe that most Aborigines are in some danger of remaining permanent victims of the past.

As Aborigines traditionally practised many difficult skills, why is it that, so often, they are treated by governments as incapable of now meeting reasonable expectations? The view that Aborigines cannot contribute adequately to the nation's well-being is also held by sections of the white population, and that belief does nothing for Aborigines' self-respect. It is almost as if there is a vicious circle of low expectations that undermines the good that is achieved by the massive subsidies directed to Aboriginal causes.

Those who doubt whether Aborigines had special skills should look at their proficiency in languages. In 1788, more languages were spoken here than in Europe. Maybe 250 different languages, most of them now silent, were spoken on this continent.

A typical Aborigine probably knew several languages and several dialects. We are inclined to downgrade this achievement by assuming that each language could be learnt in no time. But Robert Dixon, professor of linguistics at the Australian National University, insists that a typical language was complex in its grammar, being more like Latin and Sanskrit than modern English.

Dixon is an expert in the Dyirbal language, once spoken in a big area of rain-forest in north Queensland. He points out that this language clearly distinguished between him, her and it, and even had a fourth gender that a speaker used when mentioning the name of edible plants. It is sobering to realise that the grammar book of a living Aboriginal language can run to maybe 500 or more pages.

Most Aboriginal languages were complicated because, when real or potential in-laws and cousins were spoken to, another roundabout style of speaking was used. Then the nouns, adjectives and verbs could be different to those used in normal speech.

As most of us are not knowledgeable about the diversity of Aboriginal tongues, we think that Aboriginal words such as "boomerang" were once used in every corner of the land. But the same word was unlikely to be used everywhere in Australia. Thus, "kangaroo" initially came into English from the language spoken around Cooktown in north Queensland, where Captain Cook and Joseph Banks, spending time ashore, first heard the word. How to spell it was not an easy task and they wrote it down as "kanguru" or "kangooroo".

Many Aboriginal words that we still use came from the vocabulary around Sydney where native animals and Aboriginal weapons were first seen by newcomers. Words like koala, wombat, wallaby and boomerang are Sydney or Dharuk words. I assume dingo is also a Sydneyside word. It was not used at all to describe the native dog in some parts of New South Wales; and Alfred Howitt, the explorer, noted that the native dog was called Mirigang on the Shoalhaven, not far south of Sydney. Indeed, many Australian colonists were inclined to use another borrowed word, "warrigal", to describe the dog.

Such was the diversity of languages that there might well have been a total of several hundred thousand Aboriginal words, if all languages were added up. Some of the words entered the English language only recently and others will arrive later. Thus, the word "didgeridoo" was unknown to the average digger who went to Gallipoli. In far north Australia, where the musical instrument probably originated, the didgeridoo has a different name. That superb player of the instrument, Wandjuk Marika, never grew tired of telling me that his people in Arnhem Land did not call it the didgeridoo but he was too late in his plea. Rolf Harris had already won the day.

It is difficult to say so but, in my view, some Aboriginal peoples would gain more if, proud of their traditions, they sometimes demanded more of each other. That is less likely to happen, however, if government policies view them as permanent victims or puppets of a tragic past.

The Age, 13 November, 1993

IN OUR TIME

Brain-washing the Children

Many parents are astounded to learn of the Canberra edict that threatens to punish those child-care centres playing "a constant repetition of Christmas songs as background at the end of the year". Here is another instance of the attack on mainstream Australian culture at a time when Canberra praises or rewards all kinds of splinter cults and cultures.

Some parents are annoyed because the Federal Government should be minding its own business. It happens that most little children like Christmas carols. Why then should they be targets of a busybody Government?

Wondering just why the Commonwealth Government should be suspicious of Christmas music, I managed to obtain a copy of the controversial "system handbook", which expressed this suspicion. The book of more than 100 pages is called *Putting Children First*. But putting children first was the last thing the bureaucrats had in mind when they sneered at Christmas music.

The book is interesting not only for its bursts of brainwashing but because it mirrors the growth of an industry that flourishes as Australia's standard of living sags. The "long day care centre", as it is called, has multiplied to cater for the rising number of mothers who go to work. This book tells us that Australia has helped to lead the world in making "it easier for women to work", though it omits to say that Australia has also been to the fore in mismanaging its economy, with the result that more and more new mothers are forced to work because family income is too low and taxes too high and full-time male jobs too scarce.

Most of the Australian women who have little children are now in the workforce. The need for child-care centres seems to be huge. Many children, whether babies or toddlers or pre-schoolers, spend 50 hours a week and 50 weeks a year in these "long day care centres".

They are in danger of becoming weekday orphanages: and Canberra is sensibly trying to improve them and, less sensibly, to overregulate them. To continue to win a Federal subsidy, the numerous child-care centres will soon have to comply with 52 principles or at least be making progress towards them. Child-care centres have to submit to the mercies of the National Childcare Accreditation Council, or ultimately their Federal subsidy could vanish.

This book explains the 52 principles and maybe a thousand sub-principles, of which the swipe at Christmas music is one. The book has more than its share of mumbo-jumbo, including a call on the benighted staff to give "opportunities for all children to refine perceptual discrimination", whatever that means.

And yet much of the tidal wave of advice is sensible. Principle I contains 19 *don'ts,* including a warning that the staff should talk to the children as well as to each other, and a scolding for those staff who show no "interest in what children are doing or saying". It beggars belief that such elementary points have to be set down.

A host of things are disapproved of, including the practice of giving toy bulldozers only to boys and giving dolls only to girls. There is a rebuke for staff who are "only making cakes in the sandpit with girls" and "only kicking balls with boys". It is puzzling to see this advice on the same page as the rule that staff must show "sensitivity to the child-rearing practices and attitudes" of the various ethnic cultures.

There is no such sensitivity towards Christmas music. When you turn the page to see the alternative to Christmas carols, you will find just one favorable reference to a specific culture and religion. It is a call to expose little children to "the music, dance and art of Australian Aborigines and Torres Strait Islanders".

Of course, Aboriginal culture is fine when appropriate. But it is preposterous to single out the songs and art of the remote Torres Strait—what art do they have in mind?—and to discard the Christmas music so central to Western civilisation. Educators who, page after page, warn about the dangers of racial and cultural discrimination are indulging in hypocrisy when they favor a tiny minority culture and toss aside the majority culture.

They should pulp their book or add a 53rd principle which simply promises to pay a subsidy to needy mothers who prefer to stay at home rather than entrust their child to a centre of infant propaganda.

The Age, 11 December, 1993

IN OUR TIME

Casino

The opening of the Crown Casino in Melbourne is like another great swish of the windscreen wiper of morality. Victorians at the start of this century would have deplored the opening of a casino in Melbourne and would soon have toppled the government that allowed one.

Indeed, Victoria and South Australia were the states most noted for their laws against gambling, just as they were vigorous in their crusades against alcohol. Those twin crusades reached their peak in the early decades of this century, achieving their triumph with the closing of all hotels at six in the evening.

Of the strong churches in Australia, Methodism was the main opponent of gambling. Looking up the early rules of this church in Australia, I was surprised to find that there was initially no hostility to gambling. Dancing was frowned upon, wearing of costly clothes was shunned, doing any kind of business on Sunday (let alone reading a newspaper) was prohibited, and bankruptcy was especially condemned by Methodists; but gambling was not singled out as a sin.

But the popularity of horse racing and other outlets of gambling began to worry Methodists, Baptists, most Presbyterians, and members of the Church of Christ, the new Salvation Army and other evangelical Protestants. They tolerated horse racing, but not the bookmaker who took the bets.

They saw gambling as a minor form of greed. It was also socially destructive, because many Australian working men bet more money than they could afford, and their children suffered.

These attitudes might now seem narrow-minded but they had justification at the time. There was no welfare state. Public help for those in poverty was meagre. It was therefore imperative that working families saved money to prepare for any emergency, whether accident or sickness. Few obsessive gamblers earning only two pounds a week were likely to save money.

Whereas Bob Hawke as head of the trade unions enjoyed his flutter, his once-famous predecessor, W. G. Spence, denounced gambling. Spence, the first great trade unionist in Australia, led the Presbyterian Sunday School at the gold town of Creswick in the 1880s and preached at the churches of the Primitive Methodists, wagging his finger against the gamblers even though they were unlikely to be part of such a strict congregation.

Spence's hostility to gambling came not only from his religion but from his view of trade unions. They were still welfare agencies, setting up their own funds to pay for members who were sick and the funerals of those who died poor. To encourage systematic saving—in short to encourage people to manage their own lives—was part of the rationale of early trade unions.

Ninety years ago the average Victorians would probably have been stunned if they could see the betting shops in shopping centres today. Even the Post Office banned the use of its service for sending requests for lottery tickets, and the ban lasted until 1930.

Illegal back-lane betting shops flourished—John Wren ran one in Collingwood—but in 1906 the evangelicals called for the State Government to catch Wren and to suppress off-course betting.

Wesley Church in Lonsdale Street was the arsenal for this campaign, and a version of the episode is recorded in Frank Hardy's book *Power Without Glory*. The wowsers, as they were called, held a lot of political push. The Government obeyed.

By now gambling was becoming a party-political issue. Labor was more tolerant of gambling—Wren had his Labor links. On the other hand, the Liberals who dominated the Victorian Parliament were primarily Protestant and conscious that they might lose at least two dozen seats if they permitted betting of any kind outside the racecourse.

It was more difficult to gamble in Victoria and South Australia than in any other state during the period from, say, 1890 to 1950. This might seem strange because Victoria ran the country's main horse race and was the stronghold of professional running, another gambling sport.

In Victoria, legal and respectable gambling was concentrated on gold shares of the no-liability mining company—itself a Victorian invention—and sometimes on real estate. Melbourne was the hub of the wild gambling in real estate in the 1880s.

But in the eyes of evangelists there was a sharp economic distinction between the lottery ticket and the mining share. "Investment" in mining shares was vital if new mines—and thousands of jobs—were to be developed. In contrast, any jobs created in the gambling industry were seen as needless floss on the economy. There was once validity in this argument—if it was not carried too far.

In 1900 in Bendigo, 50 invested sensibly in a new gold mine floated on the local stock exchange was more important to the economy than 200 bet at the Bendigo races. Today, however, the economy is different. The tertiary sector has a new role, and gambling is not only a job-creating industry on a big scale but also a source of export income, being a potential magnet for Asian money.

New South Wales, not so evangelistic as Victoria, had originally tolerated the betting firm known as Tattersall's. "Tatt's" ran sweepstakes. The big public sweep on the Melbourne Cup in 1890 was in Sydney — there was none in Melbourne.

Indeed, in most Australian white-collar workplaces the running of a sweep on Cup day could have led to the sacking of the organiser.

Tatt's was forced out of Sydney and finally settled in Hobart where the Tasmanian Government needed revenue. Tasmania, curiously, lacks the strong Victorian tradition of suspicion of gambling. It had the first permanent public sweepstake and also, in 1973, the first casino in Australia.

Tattersall's first major task came in 1895, a lottery for the main assets of the failed Bank of Van Diemen's Land. A total of 300,000 tickets were offered for sale at one pound each — only half were sold — and the winners received prizes ranging from hotels in Hobart and Zeehan to the Devonport branch of the failed bank.

Probably nothing did more to weaken the urgency of the moral case against gambling than the rise of social security, in which Australia and New Zealand initially led the world. One by one, state governments permitted more gambling. They also enjoyed the revenue it provided.

Victoria remained wary of gambling long after NSW gave in. Victoria was a Liberal state, and, moreover, the evangelists maintained their lobby. It was that rarity, a Victorian Labor Government, which, under John Cain senior, did the unimaginable. In 1954 it invited Tatt's to move from Hobart to Melbourne.

The anti-gambling lobby was declining, but Sir Henry Bolte as Premier had to think twice about allowing off-course betting in Victoria. In May 1960 his plan for the TAB, and betting shops in the suburbs, was passed narrowly by the Legislative Assembly, but nine of his fellow Liberals and three Country Party (National) members voted against the bill.

Though the anti-gambling lobby is weak it will rise again, but not to the same heights. The welfare of children living in struggling, gambling households was the core of the concern felt a century ago, and that concern is still valid.

The Age, 16 July, 1994

The Violent

In the last few years the Western world has been taken aback by the wave of pointless shootings, including the killing of the sixteen children in a Scottish school.

On many sides the first reaction was that security measures must be introduced into schools. But how can adequate security be introduced when there are thousands of schools in Scotland and England alone and thousands of other places - whether fast food houses or entertainment parlours - where children gather in crowds?

I sometimes wonder whether we are like a doctor examining a patient suffering from measles and deciding to put a dab of whitener on each measle spot.

Significantly, one of the hallmarks of the Western world in the last 30 years is its higher emphasis on rights and lower emphasis on responsibilities. Rarely in past centuries had a society gone so far as we go in insisting that nobody is to blame for what they do. Today, when something drastically goes wrong in a human life, the excuse is instantly offered that it must really be society's fault, or the parents' fault, or the nation's fault. When the perpetrators of crimes are often encouraged to argue that they are as much the victim as the person whom they bashed or robbed or killed, then law and order are subtly undermined.

I do not wish to carry this argument too far. I am simply saying that in Western civilization, including Australia, we have probably gone too far in emphasising rights and not far enough in emphasising responsibilities.

Television stands sometimes at the centre of this conflict. A major purpose of primary and secondary education was, at one time, to offer and teach civilised role-models; but television offers other role models. The emphasis on violence and brutality seems to be reinforced by television. I read recently a study by Dr Brandon Centrewall of the School of Public

Health in the University of Washington. I do not accept his argument completely but he put forward a powerful case which the television industry should have to answer.

The introduction of television into the typical US home was parallelled by a sharp increase in the homicide rate. Between 1945 and 1974 the white homicide rate - nearly all were murders - increased by 93 per cent. Then came, from 1962, an increase in the black homicide rate which hitherto had been declining. As more black households turned to the watching of television, their homicide rate increased. In essence, the regions in the US where the viewing of television first became popular were the first regions to experience an increase in their homicide rates.

It would be wrong to see television as the sole cause - it is itself a mirror of changing values in society at large. But I wonder at the wisdom of spending huge sums on formal education in the hope of extolling good behaviour when television spends huge sums in glorifying bad behaviour, and often disseminates its opinion at the time when small children are watching.

An excerpt from the first annual lecture of the Jean Chambers Foundation, held at the Methodist Ladies' College, Kew, March 1996, which was one month before the Port Arthur shootings

Australia's Tug O' War: Europe or Asia?

1. THE ROPE TO EUROPE

Australia for most of its history was a satellite of Europe. It was settled in 1788 by the British, and in the following 180 years nearly all the immigrants came from Europe—except for an inflow of Chinese in the gold rushes. Its religion, Christianity, came directly from the British Isles, and its language too. Nearly all its technology came from Europe—until American technology contributed, once the automotive era was under way. Australia's political institutions and its system of law came from Europe. Above all, its democracy came from Europe: it is one of the oldest, continuous democracies in the world and by some definitions the oldest.

For a century and a half most of Australia's trade was with Europe. In 1914, on the eve of the First World War, Australia's imports came mainly from Europe and its exports mostly went to Europe (44 per cent to Britain and 31 per cent to Germany, Belgium and France combined).

Most Australians who went overseas for study selected Britain: the main exceptions were Germany for music and some applied sciences, and Italy for theology, and France for painting. For an Australian to study in the USA was rare before the 1950s. In the same period the foreign languages mainly studied in Australian schools were French, German, Latin and some classical Greek.

In international relations Australia, much more than did the USA, saw itself as part of Europe. It fought in the two world wars, from the very first day. Australian war deaths in Europe in the First World War exceeded those of the United States forces. Vietnam was the first war in which Australia participated not as an ally of Britain but as an ally of a non-European power, the United States.

2. THE ROPE TO ASIA

In the last quarter of a century Australia has multiplied its links with Asia, primarily East Asia. Today the majority of Australian exports go to Asia. In recent years, half of the net migration has come from Asia. Australia's largest single source of tourists is Japan, and in 1996 the biggest rate of increase in tourism was from Korea (35 per cent) and Malaysia (25 per cent). Australian universities now compete with Europe and North America for Asian students.

The teaching of Asian languages far exceeds that of European languages in Australian schools; and it is probable that an Asian language is studied by a higher proportion of children in Australia than in any nation of Europe, the Americas or Africa. Defence links with Asian nations, especially Indonesia, are probably stronger than with Europe.

This is a remarkable swing, and certainly was predicted by nobody 40 years ago. That Australia sits more easily with its neighbours, that its understanding of the diverse Asian cultures is greater, that its links with them are quickening and widening: all this is welcome.

3. RE-DRAWING THE MAP

While there has been a swing towards Asia, the official rhetoric has jumped ahead of the reality. Recently the extent and strength of the links with Asia, important and welcome as they are, have been exaggerated in Canberra's official speeches and slogans. The gestures too have become slightly inflated. The Keating Government (1991-96) emphatically proclaimed that Australia was part of Asia, and that its economic and political future lay primarily in Asia. This assertion did not cut ice amongst Asian leaders who saw Australia as friendly and near but different and definitely not Asian.

To proclaim that "Australia is part of Asia" is a vital corrective to the earlier and long-standing suspicion of Asia. But in one sense it is a half-truth. Geographically, Australia is less a part of Asia than are Greece and Russia. Likewise, Italy and Spain are very close to Africa; but in Rome and Madrid no political leader proclaims that, because of such a proximity, their own nation must jettison much of their European culture and promptly take aboard that from northern Africa. It is all a matter of proportion.

4. THE STRENGTH OF THE TWO ROPES

The strength of the present European links are overlooked by many Australian observers. In ancestry the Australian people are overwhelmingly European: the percentage is close to 90 but diminishing. Culturally, Australia's links with Europe are far stronger than with Asia. In the arts the links are much more to Europe. In sport—and sport is almost an obsession in Australia—the links are overwhelmingly with Europe and especially with Britain. Admittedly, Asian sporting links, of scant consequence in 1960, are growing.

In religion the links are overwhelmingly to Europe. The political institutions in flavour and spirit are European. So too is the law.

Tourism from Australia flows in two large streams—to Europe and to Asia. The latter is increasing because it is cheaper and because many Asian places are exotic as well as attractive. Tourists coming to Australia are increasingly from Asia. In education the link with Europe is stronger. Those Australians seeking higher education or the latest scientific knowledge available in other nations still go more to Europe and North America than to Asia.

In essence, the cultural and political and social links are far stronger with Europe. The economic links are stronger with East Asia though there are exceptions in investment and in new technology. In immigration the links with Asia are also the stronger.

5. THE FUTURE?

Australia's future does not have to lie in only one corner of the world. In economic affairs the growth of Asian links has been quick and comprehensive, but Australia's economic future might not necessarily rest with Asia as much as the present trend in statistics suggests. The world is shrinking. The international trade in services is growing more rapidly than the trade in commodities. On services the freight is cheap, and so nations far from one another can easily trade in service industries of all kinds.

It was possible, more than 100 years ago, when transport was relatively slow and expensive, for Australia to enjoy wide ranging and tight economic, cultural, and political ties with Europe. It should still be possible to hold onto many of those ties. The danger is that some of these European ties will decline unless positive steps are taken to foster them.

Spoken at a meeting of Australian and EC delegates, Brussels, September 1997

What Kind of a Republic?

I support the present mode of government in Australia, including the symbolic role of the monarchy, but I am willing to change my mind—if a superior method is put forward.

No system of government is perfect, but I am wary of supporting changes until such time as the changes, and what they will mean in practice, are carefully spelled out.

So far the republican movement has not reached a firm agreement on what it wants in place of the monarchy. The coming Convention in Canberra may clarify its mind. Even if there the republicans at last become united we cannot be sure how far their recommendations will be supported by the Federal Parliament or the final arbiter, the Australian people voting in a special referendum. The tortuous history of constitutional change suggests that republicanism could still be a long way from victory.

It is natural that great hosts of people should say instinctively that they want a republic. Moreover, their instinct has been increased by the behaviour and recent speeches of certain members of the royal family.

It is also easy for them to ask: why should we be reigned over by a monarch who does not give undivided allegiance to Australia and who does not even live in the country? There is merit in this argument, though it does overlook the facts that the Queen has probably visited more of the diverse regions of Australia than even the typical governor general when he first takes up office, that she knows more about the method of governance in Australia than maybe 95 per cent of the citizens, and that she actually exercises no political influence here.

Indeed, she could almost qualify to become an Australian citizen while remaining Queen of the United Kingdom—so lax are our citizenship laws. When the Labor Party enthusiastically altered the law in the 1980s to confer citizenship on those who knew nothing about the country, who had lived here only two years, and who wished to pursue divided loyalties, it presumably did not appreciate how much its exotic law would undermine a key republican argument that the head of state and indeed of every main office "must be filled by Australian citizens who owe their first allegiance to this country and no other".

If there is to be a President, the qualifications for office will require serious thought. Many Australians think the strict rule that the President be born here would be too restrictive, though it is the rule in the United States and Finland. On the other hand, many certainly think that a person who has lived in Australia for only a few years, and has recently sworn loyalty to another nation, should not be eligible. Curiously, the question of who should be eligible has been hardly aired in public. The debate about the republic is still in its infancy.

The broad case for a republic is not yet persuasive. The monarchy in Australia is not the same as the monarchy in England where it still has astonishing ceremonial and symbolic influence and important vestiges of political power, not least when a ministry has fallen. In Australia in effect the Queen has no power; and if she were to be seen to exercise power, that would be the end of her.

Australia has long been a republic - a crown republic - in everything but name. Some republican leaders seem reluctant to admit this because it weakens their hand when they appeal fervently to those who hardly have a clue how this country is governed. Other republicans wisely accept the truth and argue that now is the time for the final tilt of the steering wheel. But the final tilt not only has to erase the past, it has to make a new move towards the future; and that is a move into the unknown.

In essence, the proposal to turn Australia into a republic removes a symbol with virtually no power and proposes changes that will inevitably produce a new apportioning of power at the top. Mr Keating used to talk of "minimalist change" but there is faint chance of any change being minimal. In a republic, no matter what brand of a republic, the President or governor-general will have far more influence than in the past, because the position and what its incumbent says will be more important and more publicised than in the past.

The thorny questions of how the President is appointed or elected, and what powers belong to the office, will determine the attitude of many well-informed Australians who are sympathetic towards the republic. And they will cease to sympathise if those questions are not answered with skill.

A potential virtue of the forthcoming Convention is that it will acquaint public opinion with the difficulties of what seems to be such a simple question on the evening television news. And the debate might pave the way for compromises.

The creation of the Commonwealth of Australia of 1901 was as arduous a task as the creation of the republic is likely to be, and it was achieved only because the major players were willing to make compromises. Those compromises which the republican movement finally offer to its opponents will ultimately determine whether it succeeds in convincing the Australian people, for they have the last word.

Australian, 23 January, 1998

IN OUR TIME

Why the Left Will Rise Again

Communism and socialism are widely discredited, and said to be close to death. But I doubt whether even in the next half century they will fade away. It is likely that the Far Left will shake itself and regroup, marching briskly behind new banners.

Basic political ideas rise and fall. When they are rising they often seem impregnable, and when they plunge they seem about to be lost forever.

It was only 50 or so years ago that versions of socialism were said to have the world at their feet. Communist Russia was hailed as the formula for the future. George Bernard Shaw, in his brilliant and jesting way, spoke for millions of Western reformers; and in 1944 his new book *Everybody's Political What's What* proclaimed that the collective farms and garden cities of the Soviet Union were such "an immediate and enormous success" that they would soon be copied throughout the West. Stalin, he added enthusiastically, had already dotted the Russian steppes and deserts with "flourishing slumless civilized cities".

In the light of the Soviet Union's economic and social disasters, Shaw seems slightly naive today; but he was writing when most of the big cities of Europe had long contained large pockets of grimy slums as well as hosts of people who were out of work in most years of the 1930s. In contrast, there was no shortage of work in the Soviet Union in peacetime - one reason why it seemed attractive.

Moreover, capitalism itself, during the world depression, was in disarray and seemed to be in irreversible decline. John Maynard Keynes, the Cambridge genius who eventually did so much to strengthen and repackage capitalism, rang the warning bell in 1936: "It is certain that the world will not much longer tolerate the unemployment" which, in his opinion, was part and parcel of "present-day individualistic capitalism".

Even in Canberra a decade later, the leftist tide was rising high. The Chifley Labor Government began to nationalise the forerunners of the NAB and Westpac and all the private trading banks; and would have succeeded but for rearguard actions fought in the courts.

In the following decades so many of the emerging nations in the Third World experimented with various forms of socialism and communism. The ideas of English Fabians and the Left Wing Book Club fluttered down on cupped hands in Africa and India, while Marxist ideas and priorities captured China.

It was then inconceivable that these ideas, even in their strongholds, would eventually fall from favour, and that by the 1990s there would be over-excited stock exchanges in Moscow and Shanghai and that books on *How to Make Your First Million* would be hawked openly on the pavements of Prague and that free elections would be held in Hungary.

Capitalism and globalisation and the free market are now said to be the forces of the future. But their long-term victory is not assured. Nor is the total defeat and permanent humiliation of socialism inevitable.

Even in the European Union, 13 of the 15 nations are ruled by Labor or Labor-type governments. These 13 could not seriously be called socialist but some are highly interventionist. One straw in the wind is that the government which recently took office in Rome includes the first two Marxists to serve in an Italian cabinet since 1947. Likewise, in Russia and China it is far from certain that the swing away from rigid central control will continue without serious interruptions.

Sometime within the next 30 years there will be an influential relaunching of socialist and even communist ideas. Lengthy explanations - and alibis and apologies - will be offered for what went astray in the Soviet Union and China. A novel formula will try to avoid the economic blunders and political straitjacket of the old order. Perhaps the new prophets will try to do for socialism what the ingenious Keynes, with the patent help of the world depression and World War Two, did for besieged capitalism. And the resurrected socialists will strongly attack the inequalities and what they single out as the other defects of new-style capitalism.

At the same time the third world will experience, here and there, a strong revival of nationalisation with an ideology to match. The present spread of international capital creates in poor lands a rich scatter of nest-eggs which a struggling government will be tempted to confiscate, claiming that these foreign assets have been stolen from their own peoples.

Over time the reigning ideas tend to turn somersaults. There are fashions in ideas. There are periods when, for understandable reasons, a mass of people and their intellectual pilots see a solution in one set of ideas but expect far too much of them; and so those ideas are slowly deposed, giving rise to rosy expectations based often on a diametrically opposite set of ideas.

Far too much was expected of communism in Russia and China and Cuba and other nations, and too much was expected of the varieties of semi-socialism practised in Europe. In turn, too much could well be expected of capitalism and the free market which, remarkably victorious today, could easily take its victory for granted and see it as permanent.

The Age, 2 December, 1998